Buddhism

A selection of articles which serve as the key to open the
minds of people to the understanding of Buddhism from

Mahamevnawa International Meditation Centre (MIMC)
Dhammaland, Hardings Elms Road,
Billericay, Essex, CM11 2UH
England

A Mahamegha Publication

Buddhism

Ven. Kiribathgoda Gnānānanda Thero

ISBN : 978-955-687-128-9

Published July 2017

Computer Typesetting by

Mahamevnawa International Meditation Centre (MIMC)
Dhammaland, Hardings Elms Road,
Billericay, Essex, CM11 2UH, England
Telephone: 01268 533870
www.mahamevnawaimc.org

Published by

Mahamegha Publishers

Waduwawa, Yatigaloluwa, Polgahawela, Sri Lanka.
elephone: +94 37 2053300 | +94 76 8255703
mahameghapublishers@gmail.com

Printed by

Leeds Graphics (Pvt) Ltd

No. 356E, Pannipitiya Road, Thalawathugoda, Sri Lanka.
Telephone: +94 11 2801308 / +94 11 5555265

NAMO BUDDHAYA
Mahamevnawa Meditation Centre Ireland
Kilshanroe, Enfield, Kildare
Eir code: A83 TK30
FB: Buddha Meditation Ireland
FB: Mahamevnawa Meditation Centre, Republic of Ireland
www.mahamevnawa.ie
Email: info@mahamevnawa.ie
TEL : 00353 89 435 8347 / 00353 46 954 9975

Dedication

As there are lotuses that rise clear above the water and seek the nourishing beam of the sun, there are beings who seek the wisdom of the Supreme Buddha's Dhamma.

May they achieve the ultimate bliss of Nibbāna

To the Reader

Buddhism teaches the way of life, the reality of life that is ever existing in the world. The Buddha, the discoverer of this truth, directly talks about the main issue all the beings have to undergo: that is suffering. He most compassionately shows the path which leads to the end of suffering as well. He unambiguously points out that whoever earnestly practices His teachings will taste the bliss of Nibbāna, the freedom from suffering.

Countless fortunate beings who earnestly followed this unique, infallible path got liberated from what is called Samsara, the endless round of repeated births and deaths. That being the case, the Buddha's teachings are not mere words but something that becomes a reality. His teachings remain as relevant today as they were in his time twenty-six hundred years ago.

This booklet is an attempt to give readers some awareness of Buddhism. The common aim arising out of this booklet is to make readers aware of the danger of this Samsara and also the rare opportunity that the readers of this booklet are blessed with to follow the teachings of the Buddha. The content will also help the readers to understand the extraordinary qualities of the Triple Gem-the Buddha, Dhamma and Sangha-and all so to gain an understanding of profound teachings like Dependent Origination.

Mahamevnawa Buddhist monasteries compassionately offer noble friendship and guidance to all who earnestly seek knowledge and liberation in Gautama Buddha's Dispensation. For all who read this book, may the word of the Supreme Buddha enhance your wisdom.

May the noble Bhikkus and lay disciples who kindly offered suggestions and contributed to the development of this booklet be blessed by the Noble Triple Gem. And may the merits that accrue from this gift of Dhamma be lovingly transferred to our Loku Swaminwahanse, the founder of Mahamevnawa Buddhist monasteries.

"Mankind's wonderful treasure of wisdom is the Teachings of the Supreme Buddha. This Noble Doctrine, the Dhamma, illuminates our lives, bringing happiness and joy. Go in search of this wonderful Dhamma, lead your life accordingly, eradicate suffering and join that fortunate band of people who experience the Supreme Bliss"

-Venerable Kiribathgoda Gnananda Thero-

Lōkāvabōdha Suttam

The Discourse on realising the world

The discourse was taught by the Blessed One, taught by the Arahant, the fully enlightened Supreme Buddha. This is as I heard.

Monks, the world has been fully understood by the Tathāgata; the Tathāgata is detached from the world. Monks, the origin of the world has been fully understood by the Tathāgata; the origin of the world has been eradicated by the Tathāgata. Monks, the cessation of the world has been fully understood by the Tathāgata; the cessation of the world has been realized by the Tathāgata. Monks, the way leading to the cessation of the world has been fully understood by the Tathāgata; the way leading to the cessation of the world has been developed by the Tathāgata.

Monks, in the world with its devās, Māras, and Brahmas, with its recluses and brāhmins, in this whole generation with its devas and humans, whatever is seen, heard, smelled, tasted, touched, cognized, attained, sought, and reflected upon by the mind, that is fully understood by the Tathāgata. Therefore, he is called the Tathāgata.

Monks, from the night when the Tathāgata awakens to unsurpassed full enlightenment, until the night when he passes away into the Nibbāna-element with no residue left, during that time period whatever he speaks, utters, and explains, all that is just so and not otherwise. Therefore, he is called the Tathāgata.

Monks, whatever way the Tathāgata speaks, that is exactly the way the Tathāgata acts. Whatever way the Tathāgata acts, that is exactly the way the Tathāgata speaks. In this way the Tathāgata acts as He speaks and speaks as he acts. Therefore, he is called the Tathāgata.

Monks, in the world with its devas, Māras, and Brahmas, with its recluses and brāhmins, in this whole geration with its devas and humans, the Tathāgata is the conqueror of all, unvanquished, the one who realized everything, the one who took everything under his control. Therefore he is called the Tathāgata.

This is the meaning of what the Blessed One said. So with regard to this, it was said:

1.   Having realised the whole world, and the true nature of the whole world, the Tathāgata is detached from the whole world, and has abandoned desire for the whole world.

2.   The all-conquering wise sage, freed from every bond, is the Blessed One. The Buddha has reached that perfect peace, Nibbāna, which is free from fear.

3.   The Buddha is freed from all taints, and freed from all suffering with doubts destroyed, reached the destruction of all kamma, liberated by the destruction of unwholesomeness.

4.   The Enlightened One, the Blessed One, the unsurpassed lion-king, giving happiness to the world of devas and humans, turns the Noble Wheel of Dhamma.

5. *Thus, wise devās and humans went for refuge to the Buddha, and on meeting him, they pay homage: the Greatest One, the all-seeing hero.*

6. *The Blessed One is perfectly tamed: of those who tame, he is the best. The Blessed One is perfectly calmed: of those who calm others, He is the seer. The blessed One is freed from suffering: of those who free others, he is the foremost. The Blessed One crossed over samsāra: of whose help others to cross, he is the chief.*

7. *Thus, devas and humans pay homage to the Greatest One, to the all – seeing hero, saying: "In the world together with its devās there is no one equalling you. You are the unique, supreme teacher."*

NamoTassa Bhagavato Arahato Samma Sambuddhassa

Homage to the Blessed One, the Worthy One
The Supreme Enlightened One

It is good to restrain the eye; It is good to restrain the ear; It is good to restrain the nose; It is good to restrain the toungue.

Restraint in the body is good; restraint in the speech is good; restraint in the thought is good.

Restraint everywhere is good. The one restrained every where is freed from all suffering

-Dhammapada 360-361-

Table of Contents

1. Saranagamanam....................13

2. The sublime qualities of the Buddha....................17

3. The Sublime Dhamma....................28

4. The Maha Sangha....................33

5. The Rarity of the Rebirth as a Human Being....................40

6. Wrong View and Right View....................44

7. The Three Ways of Collecting Merits 49

8. The Heavenly Worlds....................69

9. Bad Destinations....................80

10. The Four Noble Truths....................85

11. Attainments of Enlightenment....................95

12. What is Kamma....................101

13. The Fortune and Misfortune of the Beings....................107

14. Spontaneous Rebirth....................114

15. Dependent Origination....................123

16. Samsara is Dangerous....................130

17. Do not Miss this Moment 137

18. Loving Kindness Meditation....................143

19. The Value of Parents....................154

20. The Noble Friend....................160

21. How the World Began – Aggañña Sutta....................165

22. Seven Suns – Saptha Sooryayuggamana Sutta....................172

Chapter One

One who has gone for refuge for the Buddha, the Dhamma and the Sangha realises with wisdom the Four Noble Truths this indeed is the safe refuge. This is the Supreme refuge. Having gone to such a refuge, one is released from all suffering.

- *Dhammapada* -

Saranāgamanam

Taking the Three Refuges

Buddham Saranam Gacchāmi
Dhammam Saranam Gacchāmi
Sangham Saranam Gacchāmi

> I go for refuge to the Supreme Buddha
> I go for refuge to the Supreme Dhamma
> I go for refuge to the Supreme Sangha

Dutiyampi Buddham Saranam Gacchāmi
Dutiyampi Dhammam Saranam Gacchāmi
Dutiyampi Sangham Saranam Gacchāmi

> For the second time I go for refuge to the Supreme Buddha
> For the second time I go for refuge to the Supreme Dhamma
> For the second time I go for refuge to the Supreme Sangha

Tatiyampi Buddham Saranam Gacchāmi
Tatiyampi Dhammam Saranam Gacchāmi
Tatiyampi Sangham Saranam Gacchāmi

> For the third time I go for refuge to the Supreme Buddha
> For the third time I go for refuge to the Supreme Dhamma
> For the third time I go for refuge to the Supreme Sangha

Buddhānussati
Recollection of qualities of the Buddha

Iti'pi so bhagavā araham, sammāsambuddho, vijjācaranasampanno, sugato, lōkavidū, anuttaro purisadammasārathi, satthā dēvamanussānam, buddho, bhagavā' ti.

Such indeed is the Blessed One; Arahant, Worthy One; Supremely Enlightened One; endowed with knowledge and virtue; follower of the Noble Path; knower of worlds; the peerless trainer of persons; teacher of gods and humans; the Enlightened Teacher; the Blessed One.

Dhammānussati
Recollection of qualities of the Dhamma

Svakkhāto bhagavatā dhammo, sanditthiko, akāliko, ēhipassiko, opanayiko, paccattam vēdittabbo viññūhi'ti.

Well taught by the Blessed One is the Dhamma, visible here and now, cannot be changed over time, open to all, self-evident, understood by the wise, each for himself.

Sanghānussati
Recollection on qualities of the Sangha

Supatipanno bhagavato sāvakasangho, Ujupatipanno bhagavato sāvakasangho, Ñāyapatipanno bhagavato sāvakasangho, Sāmīcipatipanno bhagavato sāvakasangho, Yadidam cattāri purisayugāni attha purisapuggalā ēsa bhagavato sāvaka sangho, Āhuneyyo, Pāhuneyyo,

***Dakkhineyyo, Anjalikaranīyo, Anuttaram puññakkhettam
lokassā'ti.***

Of pure conduct is the Order of Disciples of the
Blessed One. Of upright conduct is the Order of Disciples of
the Blessed One. Of wise conduct is the Order of Disciples
of the Blessed One. Of generous conduct is the Order of
Disciples of the Blessed One. Those four pairs of persons, the
eight kinds of individuals, that is the Order of Disciples of the
Blessed One. They are worthy of offerings. They are worthy
of hospitality. They are worthy of gifts. They are worthy of
reverential salutations. The incomparable field of merit for the
world.

Chapter Two

Hard is the arising of the Buddha. He is not born everywhere. Where such a great wise man is born, that clan becomes happy.

- *Dhammapada* -

The Sublime Qualities of the Supreme Buddha

The arising of a Buddha is an extremely rare happening in the world. The Buddhas do not appear frequently because the enormous amount of merit and other conditions that must be fulfilled to be a Buddha cannot be met within a short period of time. It takes aeons and aeons to fulfil the perfections (pāramita) required to be a Buddha by cultivating virtues like patience, kindness, effort, determination, morality, wisdom, selflessness and so on and even sacrificing one's belongings, body parts and life itself. Thus, a Buddha is a result of enormous power of merits accumulated through the long samsara.

The Buddha is the embodiment of all virtues. There is no other being in the human or the heavenly worlds who is similar to the Buddha in noble qualities. He has the highest morality (Sila), deepest concentration (Samādhi) and the highest wisdom (Pañña). The Buddha is known as "asama" meaning "not similar to anyone". A Buddha is similar only to another Buddha and therefore is known as *"asama-sama"*.

He is neither a myth nor a god. He was born as a human, a crown prince, in India about 2600 years ago with the name, Siddharta. He married a princess called Yasodhara at the age of sixteen and had a son named Rahula. At the age of twenty-nine prince Siddharta left the home life and went into homelessness in search of the Truth and became enlightened by the name of Gautama Buddha, at the age of thirty-five, under the Bodhi Tree at Gaya, India. During a forty-five-year ministry, a countless number of humans and gods realised the Truth and attained Nibbāna through His teachings while many more were fortunate enough to become liberated from ever being reborn in the four lower destinations* forever. The Buddha passed away at the age of eighty at Kusinara.

A Buddha appears in the world to rescue beings from suffering by eradicating its cause and to teach a way to put an end to both birth and death.

He preaches neither puzzles, riddles nor dogmas which one must blindly believe, nor a creed or faith which one must accept without reasoning. His teachings are practical, understandable and realistic. What He taught was the nature of life that is hidden in the darkness of ignorance. He realised everything fully in its true nature and His knowledge was not covered by anything. There are no secrets or mysteries that are beyond His comprehension. His knowledge was so much that once while in a forest He gathered a few leaves in his hand and said to the monks that the things that He taught were comparable to the amount of leaves in His hand and what He did not teach was comparable to the amount of leaves in the forest. He taught only what is necessary to gain freedom from suffering.

(Simsapa Sutta - SN 5)

The Supreme Buddha's kindness and compassion extended to all beings were boundless. He tried His best to rescue beings from suffering. Sometimes He walked hundreds of miles a day looking for helpless and wise men and women to bring about their spiritual welfare. Therefore, He was

---

*Described in Chapter nine.

known as "Maha Karuniko, the Great Compassionate One". Because of His highest morality (Sila), deepest concentration (Samadhi), great wisdom (Pañña) and other immeasurable qualities the Buddha is known as "agga-dakkineyyo", the most suitable one for offerings. Even today, any offering whether it be food, drinks, medicine, flowers, lamps, incense etc. made in homage to the Buddha with a pleasant mind will yield incalculable and immeasurable merits.* Furthermore, the veneration, homage and respect paid to Him by recollecting his great qualities produce lots of merits to one's life. There is no one in the world who can fully understand the qualities of a Buddha other than another Buddha. Even an Arahant -an enlightened disciple of the Buddha- cannot do that. It is said that if a Buddha were to recite the qualities of another Buddha for an aeon, there would be many more qualities still left to be recited at the end of that aeon.

However in His great wisdom and compassion, the Supreme Buddha taught nine sublime qualities of the Buddha for gods and humans to contemplate, as a subject of meditation and to recite when paying homage.

Araham

'Araham' is the first quality that the Buddha taught us so that we could identify who a Buddha is. The quality Araham means that the Supreme Buddha is an Arahant. The Buddha is the first Arahant in the world.

The Buddha completely eradicated desire, hatred and delusion for good and when He became an Arahant, He is

---

*Described in Chapter seven

free from defilements like anger, pride, jealousy and the like. Therefore, He has an extremely pure mind that is not affected by anything that arouses the mind. Also, the Buddha is called Arahant because He purified His body, speech and mind. His sense faculties – eye, ear, nose, tongue, body and mind - are well restrained since He has tamed them forever. Therefore, the Supreme Buddha is peaceful, serene, contended, happy and delighted. No one can make Him scared as He got rid of fear when he became an Arahant. In addition to that, the Supreme Buddha is called 'araham' because He, is worthy of offerings of all the gods and humans just because He generated in His mind all the wholesome qualities and eliminated all the unwholesome qualities from His mind.

Sammā Sambuddho

The second quality, 'Samma Sambuddho' implies the meaning, self attainment. Every one of us has teachers who teach us how to live in the society, how to pass an examination, etc. We have to read at least a book to get to know something, but the Supreme Buddha had no teachers to teach Him how to attain the Buddhahood. It is true that before the enlightenment He went to the teachers like Ālāra-Kālāma and Uddaka Rāmputta to learn a way that leads to Nibbāna, but the Bōdhisatta (the Buddha-to-be) understood that they could teach only deep levels of concentration which only lead to rebirth in higher divine worlds which was not his ultimate goal. Then He decided to seek the truth on his own. Finally, He discovered the Noble Eightfold Path and attained Nibbāna by realising the four Noble Truths without any guidance from anyone or referring to any book. The Buddha realised the noble truth of suffering, the noble truth of cause for suffering, the noble truth of the end of suffering and the noble truth of the way leading to the end of suffering. For that reason, the Supreme Buddha is designated as 'Samma Sambuddho'.

Vijjācharana Sampanno

This quality 'Vijjācarana Sampanno' is of two aspects. One is 'Vijja' which means vision or knowledge. Basically the Supreme Buddha has Three-fold knowledge called 'Tevijja' in Pali language. The first is the knowledge of recollecting the past lives of the Buddha himself and that of others. In an instant, He can trace back manifold previous lives. The second is the knowledge of being able to see beings passing away and reappearing. By way of this knowledge, He can see how beings who commit unwholesome deeds by mind, body and speech are born in bad destinations and those who accumulate wholesome deeds are born in heavenly worlds. The third is the knowledge of the destruction of the taints or defilements. That is, He knows that he is liberated from all unwholesome states and that he is an Arahant.

In addition to the threefold knowledge, the Supreme Buddha has psychic powers like travelling in the air like birds, diving in and out of the earth as though it was water, walking on water without sinking as though it was earth, touching, stroking the sun and moon, going unhindered through a wall or a mountain as through space and so on. And also connected with the aspects of Vijja, the Supreme Buddha had the following abilities:

1. He could hear both kinds of sounds, the divine and the human, those that are far as well as near.

2. He could read the minds of other beings, of other persons.

3. He could see with his divine eye anything and any living being like gods, ghosts and other non-human beings, and talk with them.

4. He could understand whether beings can realise Dhamma or not and in which ways they are made to realise Dhamma.

The second aspect of this quality is 'charana' which means good conduct. It also means that the Buddha lived His life according to the above mentioned vijja, the eightfold knowledge. 'Charana' that he was endowed with is manifested by his perfect morality, mindfulness, concentration, contentment, wakefulness, patience, diligence and liberation.

Sugathō

The fourth quality, 'sugathō' means that the path the Supreme Buddha followed is extremely pleasant, good and excellent. The path is the Noble Eightfold Path which is the one and only way that leads to Nibbāna, the freedom of suffering. The Supreme Buddha is the first to discover this pleasant path and attain the pleasant Nibbāna. Therefore, he is designated as 'sugato' 'the one who followed the pleasant path'.

Lōkavidu

The term 'Lōkavidu' is applied to the Supreme Buddha as the one with sharp and perfect knowledge of the world. He knows the world like the back of his hand. There were no secrets about any world for him. We humans know this world and have discovered some other planets, using modern technology, but we know only a little even about this world. But the Supreme Buddha with His divine eye saw that there are many more worlds and thousands of world-systems and beings living there. He, having fully known, taught us information about heavenly worlds, higher mode of heavenly realms called brahma worlds, hell worlds, ghost worlds and asura world in addition to this human world and the animal world, the two worlds that we know and see with our own eyes. All that we know about worlds is something round that we call a planet, but the Supreme Buddha interpreted the world as a place with life.

The quality '*Lokavidu*' means 'fantastic and marvellous'. He said that there are many hundred thousands of world systems and He could talk with beings conveying his voice as far as he wanted. In His words, He sends a beam of light to the faraway world systems and when those beings see that light, He projects His voice and makes them hear the sound.

(Abhibhu Sutta - AN 1)

Also the Supreme Buddha preached that beings are moving from world to world according to the kamma accumulated by them. Those who accumulate good kamma are reborn in heavenly and brahma worlds and those who accumulate bad kamma are reborn in lower worlds like hell, ghost world and animal world while those who accumulate both good and bad kamma are reborn in the human world. Those who completely eradicate all good and bad kamma get liberated from all the worlds.

The Supreme Buddha preached how this material world one day will end and how it will be formed again. The Supreme Buddha also understood the origin of the spiritual world (worlds of eye, ear, nose, tongue, body and mind.), its cessation and the path to the cessation thereof and escaped from all the worlds. Therefore, the Supreme Buddha is called *'Lokavidu'*, the knower of the worlds.

Anuttaro Purisa-Damma Sārathi

'Anuttaro Purisadamma Sarathi' means 'the incomparable leader of men to be tamed'. The Supreme Buddha tamed not only humans, but also gods, brahmas and ferocious demons like Ālavaka. Sometimes, he tamed giant elephants like Nālagiri who was sent to kill Him. He tamed beings without using any weapons but instead with His great wisdom and compassion. Sometimes He tamed beings by means of His psychic powers. Not only did He tame human and heavenly beings but He also showed them the way to the liberation from suffering. Even though the Buddha is no more today, the Dhamma, the teachings He used to subdue people, has that power of taming those who listen to it even now. It is because of that power that people who listen to Dhamma try to give up greed and become generous, to get rid of misconduct by mind, body and speech. And also, they become virtuous and control the mind and purify it from defilements.

Sattā Dēva Manussānam

The seventh quality, *'Sattā deva manussanam'* means that the Supreme Buddha is the teacher of gods and humans.

He was a universal teacher. He was such a great teacher that He could give the real solution to any problem of gods and humans. The solutions of this great teacher were to the point and most of the time that solution resulted in the eternal bliss of Nibbāna. The Supreme Buddha was a unique teacher who was concerned not only about the worldly well being but also about the spiritual well-being of gods and humans.

As a religious teacher, He encouraged gods and humans to think freely without depending on religious beliefs. He never used fear as a means of converting people to His teachings. He introduced a very practical religious way of life for people to be religious even without a religious label.

Buddho

The Supreme Buddha is named '*Buddho*' because He taught the Dhamma that he realised to others so that they too could realise it. He preached the Dhamma very pleasantly and very clearly with different words, different meanings and diverse techniques suited to the different mentalities of gods and human beings.

Bhagavā

The ninth quality '*Bhagavā*' means 'the Fortunate One'. He was fortunate to have an extremely pure heart devoid of defilements and he was fortunate enough to understand the Four Noble Truths without any advice or guidance from any teacher or instructor. Also the Supreme Buddha was fortunate to have unlimited knowledge and great wisdom as well as the deepest concentration. Furthermore, he was the most fortunate among the mankind for being endowed with supernormal powers and an exquisitely beautiful body consisted of thirty - two special marks. Briefly, the Supreme Buddha was fortunate to have a pure heart which contained all the supreme qualities and superhuman abilities. For those reasons, Supreme Buddha is designated as 'Bhagava', the most Fortunate One.

Chapter Three

The person who lives by the Dhamma is protected by the Dhamma itself just as one is holding a big umbrella in the rain. This is the benefit of practising the Dhamma. One who lives by the Dhamma does not go to hell.

- The arahant Dhammika -

The Sublime Dhamma

The Supreme Buddha became enlightened under the Bodhi Tree at Gaya and with His Enlightenment he realised the truth ever prevailing in the universe. He, with great compassion, taught the truth discovered by him to both human and heavenly beings, which became his teachings, the teachings of the Buddha. The Supreme Buddha by himself referred to what he realised and what he taught as Dhamma. **So, the term Dhamma is not used for anything other than the teachings of the Supreme Buddha or the reality which he understood.**

Through this Dhamma, the Supreme Buddha taught how to see things as they really are which are clouded by avijja, (ignorance). Also, it is the Supreme Buddha's Dhamma that makes us aware of the fact that samsara, the continuous process of being born, growing old and dying again and again, is extremely dangerous. And also, this Sublime Dhamma teaches us that there are other worlds where beings are reborn such as heavenly worlds where there is happiness and lower worlds where there is extreme suffering. This Dhamma also enlightens us with the fact that rebirth as a human is extremely rare, and most of the time beings are bound to be reborn in lower worlds like hell according to the action (kamma) they commit. What is special about this noble Dhamma is that it teaches how to avoid lower worlds and how to be reborn in heavenly worlds and how to get rid of suffering completely by living according to that Dhamma itself. The unique discovery revealed by this Dhamma is that everything is a result of a 'cause'. According to that theory, we are the result of what we were, and we will be the result of what we are.

This Dhamma realised by the Blessed One has many virtues or qualities. Among the many virtues or qualities, there are six salient characteristics mentioned by the Supreme Buddha. These particular Dhamma qualities are chanted by Buddhists during their devotional observances. The popular Pāli verse presenting these Dhamma qualities is as follows.

Svākkāto Bhagavata Dhammo, Sandittiko, Akāliko, Ēhipassiko, Ōpanayiko, Paccattam Vēditabbo Viññuhi

An explanation of these six Dhamma qualities is given here:-

1.Svākkāto Bhagavata Dhammo

The term 'Svakkāta' is a joint word. They are 'Su' and 'Akkata'. The term 'Su' in pali is well and the word 'akkkāta' means 'preached' or 'expounded'. Then the full meaning of the word 'Svakkāta' is 'well-preached' or 'well-expounded'. The Dhamma is well expounded by the Supreme Buddha. It is excellent at the beginning, excellent in the middle and excellent at the end. Just as every drop of water in the ocean has only one taste; the taste of salt, the Dhamma has only one taste; the taste of Nibbāna. It is because the Dhamma is well preached without any contradiction; there is no room for anyone to deviate from it. Therefore, the one who follows the path of Dhamma confidently, diligently and continuously will definitely succeed in attaining Nibbāna* one day.

2. Sandittiko

This quality 'Sandittiko' is an outstanding characteristic of the Dhamma. It means that the intended result can be

---

*Described in Chapter eleven

experienced within this life itself if the Dhamma is learned well and put into sincere practice diligently. The followers of this Dhamma do not have to wait for the next life to know the result therein. So, the beneficial results of this Dhamma is visible here and now because it has been 'well-preached by the Blessed One'. If one, for instance, wishes for his or her anger to be abandoned, the perfect medicine is prescribed by the Dhamma in a way that he or she can get to know for himself or for herself that anger is under his or her control. If need be, one can completely eradicate anger within this life itself depending on the attempt put forth and the power of his merits and the capacity of his wisdom.

3.Akāliko

The Dhamma, the teaching of the Supreme Buddha, is not a revelation or a speculation but it is the unwavering absolute truth ever existing in the world. The nature of truth is that it is never subject to any change from time to time, and does not become invalid as time goes by. Therefore, this Dhamma can be realised at any time because it always remains valid.

4.Ēhipassiko

The Dhamma is open to anyone, and therefore it makes an open invitation to all to come and see it. This Dhamma is not something that you can foist on someone. Instead, you can invite someone to come and see without any fear but with great confidence because there is nothing mysterious about it.

Specifically, this Dhamma is pure and crystal clear. It is as pure as solid gold. That is why, anyone can be invited to come and see it without any doubt and fear. Anyone has the freedom whether to follow it or not. That is why, the Dhamma is of the quality 'Ēhipassika'. 'Ēhipassika', come and see, marks the greatness of the Supreme Buddha who is the discoverer of this Sublime Dhamma.

5. *Ōpanayiko*

The term 'Ōpanayiko' means that the results or the benefits of the Dhamma should be experienced within the one who follows it. No one can come to a conclusion that such and such is the Dhamma unless one follows it and lives by it and gets to know the results himself. That being the case, following the Dhamma is something personal, not something that can be seen through others who follow it.

6.*Paccattam Vēditabba Viññuhi*

There are two significant aspects of this phrase. The first is that the result or the benefits intended is to be acquired individually as is meant by 'Paccattam' and secondly, the Dhamma is understood only by the wise. According to the quality, 'Paccattam Vēditabbo Viññuhi' implies that the Dhamma is to be understood individually by the wise. One's attainment of enlightenment cannot be exchanged with another or one cannot pass one's wisdom acquired through the Dhamma on to someone else. The follower of this Dhamma has to experience the blessings or virtues of it by himself according to his wisdom.

Chapter Four

Happy is the arising of the Buddhas, happy is the teaching of the Dhamma, happy is the unity of the Sangha, happy is the meditation of such united ones.

- Dhammapada -

The Noble Maha Sangha

The term 'Sangha' refers here to the Supreme Buddha's ordained disciples. They are known as Bhikkhus (or Buddhist monks) and Bhikkhunis* (or Buddhist nuns). They have left their household life and are homeless. They have dedicated their life to the great teacher, the Supreme Buddha and His noble Dhamma with the noble intention of putting an end to suffering. They have shaved their heads and wear robes. They depend on the robes, alms, dwellings and medicine offered by the lay disciples of the Supreme Buddha. The Sangha serves as a field of blessings and a channel for spreading the Supreme Buddha's teachings to the lay community. The lay community is responsible for providing the material needs of the Bhikkhus. In doing so, they are expected to act with proper etiquette, saluting the Bhikkhus respectfully, offering them a seat, giving generously, and showing good care for their well being.

The noble Sangha is obliged to provide an inspiring model of disciplined conduct to the lay people, behaving in such a way that "those without confidence gain confidence and those with confidence increase in their confidence". They keep the highest Sīla (virtue). The novice monks observe ten precepts (disciplinary rules) before higher ordination and higher ordained monks observe 227 precepts and more minor precepts. While they have observed higher precepts, they try to inculcate good human values and qualities in their minds

---

*Female ordained disciples

as a strong foundation for meditation. The heart of monastic life is the practice of meditation, the effort to tame and master the mind. Therefore, one of the significant aspects of the daily routine of Buddhist monks is to develop his mind by means of meditation in order to see things as they really are. The ultimate goal of the monastic life of the Bhikkhus is to purify their minds from defilements and attain Arahantship. The Maha Sangha comprised of Arahants is of infinite qualities because of their Sīla (virtue), Samādhi (concentration) and Pañña (wisdom).

In one of his sermons, the Supreme Buddha pointed out the holiness and greatness of the noble Sangha thus;

> *"To what extent there are Sanghas or groups, the Sangha of the Tathagata's disciples is declared the foremost among them... Those who have confidence in the Sangha have confidence in the foremost, and for those who have confidence in the foremost, the result is foremost."*

An explanation of the Pali verse with which the Buddhist devotees pay homage to the noble Sangha is given below:

Supatipanno Bhagavato Sāvakasangho, Ujupatipanno Bhagavato Sāvakasangho, Ñāyapatipangno Bhagavato Sāvakasangho, Sāmicipatipanno Bhagavato Sāvakasangho, Yadidam chattāri purisayugāni atta purisa puggala ēsa Bhagavato Sāvakasangho, Āhuneyyo, Pāhuneyyo, Dakkhineyyo, Anjalikaranīyo, Anuttaran puññakkhettam lokassāti.

Supatipanno Bhagavato Sāvakasangho

This phrase conveys that the order of disciples of the Blessed One is of pure conduct. They live the monastic life in order to eradicate lust, hatred, and delusion which are the primary causes for suffering. When they practise Dhamma with that intention, they refrain from doing anything wrong and inappropriate by the three doors, that is; mind, body and speech.

Ujupatipanno Bhagavato Sāvakasangho

The path that the order of disciples follow is an upright one (straight one) which leads to Nibbāna itself. That is the Noble Eightfold Path. There is no likelihood that they could deviate from this straight path if they follow it exactly as the Buddha has taught. And also, they have this quality, Ujupatipanna, because their sole ambition is none other than getting liberated from suffering, that is, attaining Nibbāna.

Ñāyapatipanno Bhagavato Sāvakasangho

Ñāyapatipanno means that the order of the disciples of the Blessed One follow the path in order to develop wisdom which enables them to realise the Four Noble Truths: suffering, the origin of suffering, the end of suffering, and the path leading to the end of suffering.

Sāmicipatipanno Bhagavato Sāvakasangho

This quality 'Sāmicipatipanno' conveys the meaning that the Sangha is of talk which leads to understanding, wisdom and enlightenment; that is talk about fewness of wishes, talk about contentment, talk about seclusion, talk about not getting bound up with others, talk about arousing energy, talk about virtuous behaviour, talk about concentration, talk about wisdom, talk about liberation, and talk about the knowledge and vision of liberation. The noble Sangha who is endowed with these ten talks teaches the Dhamma to others with compassion. The noble service they render by spreading the message of the Supreme Buddha to the world is tremendous and invaluable. Because of the noble Sangha who spread the Dhamma, the lay people get the opportunity to accumulate merits and to be reborn in a heavenly world and to realise the Dhamma (to attain Nibbāna).

Yadidam chattāri purisayugāni atta purisa puggalā ēsa Bhagavato Sāvakasangho

The noble Sangha of the Blessed One consists of eight types of noble persons and when coupled there are four pairs. The two members of each pair are the one who has attained the stage itself and the one who has entered the path leading irreversibly towards that stage. They are: "The stream-enterer, the one practising for the realisation of the fruit of stream-entry, the Once-returner, the one practicing for realisation of the fruit of once-returning, the non-returner, the one practicing for realisation of the fruit of non-returning, the Arahant, the one practising for realisation of the fruit of Arahantship."

Āhuneyyo

This means that the noble Sangha is worthy of offering. Because of the great qualities and virtues they have, it is worth travelling many miles to offer them food, drinks, medicine, etc.

Pāhuneyyo

'Pāhuneyyo' denotes that the noble Sangha is worthy of hospitality. When they visit a house (asking for alms food etc) they are worth receiving what they need at the time.

Dakkhineyyo

This quality, 'Dakkineyyo' means that the noble Sangha is worthy of gifts. They deserve to be given food, robes, medicine, dwellings and other requirements on account of their great qualities they hold. Whatever little they are given with a pleasant mind produces great fruits and benefits.

Anjalikaraniyo

'Anjalikaraniyo' implies the meaning that the Blessed One's order of the disciples is worthy of reverential salutations. They should be respected by standing up, offering a seat, paying homage, worshipping them with five fold rest and fulfilling respective duties. It is improper to sit on a chair or any other lofty seat unless you are ill while the noble monks are standing or preaching Dhamma. The lay devotees sit close by on a lower seat than the venerable monk's to listen to the Dhamma.

Anuttaran puññnakkhettam lokassāti

This quality means that the noble Sangha is the incomparable field of merit for the world. Lay people can gain enormous merit by giving them robes, alms food, dwellings and medicine. The merits accumulated will result in extraordinary happiness for a long time. The Supreme Buddha preached that the result (merit) of the offering made in the name of noble Sangha is immeasurable and incalculable just as the water in the great ocean cannot be measured. One can also gain merits by offering a seat, saluting, paying homage and developing a pleasant mind by seeing them. The noble Sangha is of course a field of merit for the world and therefore anyone can reap "a great harvest of merit by planting seeds of 'giving' in that field of merit."

Chapter Five

It is hard to be born as a human being. Hard is the life of
human beings. It is hard to gain the opportunity to hear the
Dhamma and seldom is the appearance of the Buddhas.

- Dhammapada -

The Rarity of Rebirth as a Human Being

The human life is exceedingly rare and hard to obtain again and again. Once one is reborn in one of the bad destinations, it is extremely difficult to regain the human state. The Buddha described that difficulty by giving the simile of the one eyed turtle.

"Bhikkhus, suppose that this great earth has become one mass of water, and a man throws a yoke (log) with a single hole upon it. When the wind comes from the east, the log drifts westwards, when the winds blow from the west, it drifts eastwards. Similarly, the north winds push it to the south and the south winds push it to the north. In this ocean, there is a one eyed turtle that comes to the surface once in every hundred years. What do you think, Bhikkus, will that one eyed turtle, coming to the surface once in every hundred years, insert its neck into that yoke with a single hole?"

"If it would ever do so Venerable Sir, it would be only after a very long time. It would be rarely that a chance might occur", then the Buddha explained,

"Monks, this rare chance, this freak occurrence is possible, but for an unwise person who is reborn in a bad destination, to become a human being again is much rarer and much more difficult. For what reason-It's because in the lower realms there is no conduct guided by the Dhamma, no righteous conduct, no wholesome activity, no meritorious activity. They pray upon each other- the strong hunting the weak."

(Chiggala Sutta - SN 5)

The Buddha explains why they have to suffer that way in the lower worlds. It is because they have not realised the Four Noble Truths. The above account shows us how rare and how precious the rebirth as a human being is.

One may think that the number of human beings is more than that of animals or other beings in the worlds. One normally tends to think so because of one's utter delusion or lack of knowledge about the world. When compared to the number of all animals, the number of human beings is very few. The number of ants in a few ant nests alone is far greater than that of the human beings. Not to mention about the number of other animals on land. Even greater than these animals are the visible creatures in the four great oceans. It is mentioned in the Dhamma that the number of the invisible creatures in the oceans is countless. It is said that the most beings live in the hell world known as 'Avichi'; the place of sinners who have committed the five grave offences* and other very serious sinful deeds.

According to these facts, the human life is exceedingly rare. It is rarely that a being who is wandering and roaming in this long samsara gets an opportunity to be reborn as a human being. Though we see that human beings are born in thousands every day, they have come to this human world after having suffered in lower worlds over a long period of time (sometimes for aeons). Also, from among the humans

---

Five grave offences:*

    1.Killing one's own mother   2.Killing one's own father
    3.Depriving an Arahant of life
    4.Shedding a blood of a Buddha with a hateful mind
    5.Schism (creating a division amongst the noble Sangha)

who pass away, most of them are reborn in lower worlds again. On one occasion, The Blessed One took up a little bit of soil in his finger nail and addressed the bhikkus thus,

"What do you think, bhikkus, which is more: the little bit of soil on my finger nail or the great earth?"

"Venerable Sir, the great earth is more. The little bit of soil that the Blessed One has taken up on his fingernail is trifling. Compared to the great earth, the little bit of soil that the Blessed One has taken up on his finger nail is not calculable, does not bear comparison, does not amount even to a fraction."

"So too, Bhikkus, those beings are numerous who, when they pass away from the human world, are reborn in hell...in the animal realm...in the domain of ghosts..."

(Manussacuti Sutta - SN 5)

Only a few of human beings get the rare chance to listen to the Dhamma by the Buddha who rarely appears in the human world and to learn the right view of the things and to live accordingly. Only those human beings are fortunate to be reborn as a human being or as a heavenly being again.

Therefore, we humans should well understand the value of the human state and try to enhance the human qualities, thereby have another opportunity to be reborn in a good destination. Therefore, we should be determined to protect our precious life from unwholesome activities which lead to suffering. We should develop good human qualities according to the Buddhist teachings, and do as many meritorious deeds as possible by means of dāna (generosity), sīla (virtue) and bhāvanā (meditation) with the intention of realising the Four Noble Truths.

Chapter Six

Those who consider the noble Dhamma as wrong and the wrong (views) as right, upholding wrong views go to hell.

Having known wrong things as wrong and right things as right, upholding right views, these people go to heaven.

- *Dhammapada* -

Wrong View and Right View

Wrong View

The Supreme Buddha taught that there are two views found existing in the world. They are Right View and Wrong View. Out of the two, Wrong View is extremely dangerous. It is Wrong View that is spread everywhere in the world. Wrong View consists of ten issues:

1. There are no results in giving.
2. There are no results in helping and giving service to others.
3. There are no results in veneration and making offerings.
4. There are no fruit and result in good and bad actions (kamma).
5. There is no place called, 'this world',
6. There is no place called other world (there is no life after death).
7. There is no special person called mother.
8. There is no special person called father.
9. There are no beings who are born spontaneously,
10. There are no good and virtuous recluses and brahmins in the world who have realised this world and the other world by themselves through their own knowledge.

The person who holds on to these ten subjects of Wrong View is called the holder of Wrong View. Wrong View is the worst thing that is blameworthy. For a person of

Wrong View, there is no evil that cannot be committed. The Supreme Buddha taught that for a person of Wrong view, whatever bodily kamma, verbal kamma and mental kamma he does and undertakes in accordance with that Wrong View, all leads to disaster, harm and suffering. "Suppose, a seed of neem, bitter cucumber or bitter gourd were planted in moist soil. Whatever nutrients it takes up from the soil and from the water would all lead to its bitter, pungent and disagreeable flavour. Why is that? Because the seed is bad". The Supreme Buddha explained, "So too, for a person of Wrong View, whatever kamma he does bodily, verbally and mentally, all lead to disaster, harm and suffering."

(AN 1)

Because of Wrong View, unarisen unwholesome qualities arise, and arisen unwholesome qualities increase and expand. And also, unarisen wholesome qualities do not arise and arisen wholesome qualities decline on account of Wrong view. Therefore, it seems that all the well-being and happiness of a person can be completely obstructed by Wrong View. 'Wrong Views' are taught in the name of religion from time to time in the world. Terrorism is caused by Wrong View itself. The Supreme Buddha said, 'There is one person who arises in the world for the harm of many people, for the unhappiness of many people, for the ruin and suffering of many people of devas (gods) and human beings. Who is that one person? It is one who holds Wrong View and has incorrect attitudes. He draws many people away from the good Dhamma and establishes them in a bad Dhamma'.

(AN 1)

The danger that lies in Wrong View is that once one begins to believe a Wrong View and is conditioned in accordance with it, it is extremely difficult for him to get rid of that Wrong View. He tenaciously holds on to the Wrong View and he thinks that the view held by him is the truth and all other views are wrong. Such a person, blinded by wrong views, is prepared to do anything, even to kill others as a suicide bomber. Therefore, "there is not a single thing that is very dangerous, and harmful so much as Wrong View".

(AN 1)

A holder of Wrong View is destined to be reborn in two lower worlds after death just because of his view. They are hell and the animal world.

Right View in Ten Issues

It is the Right View in ten issues that basically enables a person to be reborn in the human world or in the heavenly worlds. In Buddhism, two Right Views are mentioned, namely: the Mundane or worldly Right View and the Supermundane Right View. The former leads to generating the latter which arises in the Noble Eightfold Path. It is a person of the Right View in ten issues who believes kamma and its results as well as the Buddhas who teach the way leading to Nibbāna. The ten issues that belong to the Mundane Right View are:

1. There are results in giving

2. There are results in helping and giving services to others.

3. There are results in veneration and making offerings.

4. There are fruits and results in good and bad actions (kamma).

5. There is a place called 'this world'.

6. There is a place called 'other world' (there is a life after death).

7. There is a special person called mother.

8. There is a special person called father.

9. There are beings who are born spontaneously.

10. There are good and virtuous recluses & bramins in the world who have realised this world and the other world by themselves through their own knowledge.

The Supreme Buddha taught that for a person of Right View, whatever bodily kamma, verbal kamma and mental kamma he does and undertakes according to that Right View all leads to welfare, betterment and happiness. "Suppose, a seed of apple was planted in moist soil. Whatever nutrients it takes up from the soil and from the water would all lead to its sweet, delicious and agreeable flavour. Why is that? Because the seed is sweet". The Supreme Buddha explained, "so too, for a person of Right View, whatever kamma he does bodily, verbally and mentally all lead to welfare, betterment and happiness".

(AN 1)

So it is a great blessing and great fortune for a person to believe the Right View which determines all his happiness.

Chapter Seven

When, after a long absence, a man safely returns home from afar, his relatives, friends, and well-wishers welcome him home on arrival.

As relatives welcome a dear one on arrival, even so his own meritorious deeds will welcome the doer of good who has gone from this world to the next.

- Dhammapada -

Three Ways of Accumulating Merits

The word 'merit' is widely discussed in Buddhism. 'Merit' is an abstract thing generated in one's life when one acts by means of body, speech and mind in a way that leads to welfare and happiness to both oneself and others. For instance, one having seen an ant fallen on water, saves its life and frees it from fear. So that good act generates merits which will result in happiness to be experienced either in this life itself or in a future existence. If someone acts by body, speech and mind and then not regret but delights in the virtue of the moral quality of the act, it is considered as an act of merit.

'Merit' is what that leads to the happiness of all beings - gods and humans. Where there are merits, there is happiness. 'Person' is a creation of merits. If a person enjoys a lot of happiness, it means he has accumulated a lot of merit in his previous lives. Those who collect merit are born in good worlds like heavenly worlds and this human world. Those who accumulate demerits are likely to be reborn in bad worlds such as hell, the animal world etc. One who accumulates merit is protected by merit itself. One who has little or no merit has to undergo lots of hardships. Even in this human world, there is a huge difference among people because of the difference of merits.

The Supreme Buddha compared merit to a treasure. No one can give the treasure of merits to someone else hand in hand as it is an invisible thing. Any material wealth one possesses can be stolen by thieves, but the merits can never be stolen by anyone. That treasure of merits follows the owner

when he leaves this world just as one's shadow comes after I
wherever he goes. When a man leaves this world, he car
take anything with him but only the merits he has gained

The Supreme Buddha said that because of the trea
of merits one gets a beautiful appearance, a melodious vo
a well-shaped body, a higher social status and good pe
around him who provide help and support. Furtherm
the Buddha said local kingships, agreeable happiness
universal monarch, human and heavenly happiness
all comforts are received because of the power of m
previously accumulated. The supreme Buddha stressec
importance of collecting merit not only because it leads t
happiness of beings but also it enables us to attain Nibl
the freedom of suffering. If a person who is trying to a
Nibbāna has a huge mass of merits, the external hindra
which disturb his attempts could be avoided by the p
of his merits. He could reach the goal with ease as the i
makes the environment conducive to him in every way
supreme Buddha has pointed out that there are three wa
collecting merits:

1.   Dāna (Giving)
2.   Sīla (Morality)
3.   Bhāvana (Meditation)

Dāna (Giving)

Dāna is one of the ways of collecting merits.
or being generous is also one of the noble human qu
that we can cultivate in ourselves. Dāna means that w
away things that belong to us for the betterment, welfa

happiness of others in need. Dāna includes things such as food, drinks, clothes, medicine, stationery, vehicles, houses, lights and anything that one needs. The Buddha appreciated the act of giving very much. He said that by giving some food even to an animal one can earn hundreds of results and that one gains much more benefits by giving alms food to a human being. He further taught that the amount of merit that is generated by giving alms to the Supreme Buddha and His disciples- the Mahā Sangha - cannot be calculated and measured. The order of disciples of the Blessed One is worthy of offerings. The Supreme Buddha said, 'They are the incomparable field of merit for the world'.

When we give food and drinks to someone, we give him five things namely; life span, complexion, happiness, power (strength) and ability to think wisely. The giver will receive the same in return either in the human world or in a heavenly world. We need to remember to offer food or anything with our own hands with a pleased mind as well as with much respect towards those who receive them. Furthermore, we should not forget to pay homage to venerable monks and elderly people when we give something to them. The Supreme Buddha taught how a good person should give something whether it be food, drinks, clothes, etc. to another.

1. He gives in an orderly manner.
2. He gives respectfully.
3. He gives with his own hands.
4. He gives what would not
5. He gives in faith of k

If we have everything that a man needs such as foods, drinks, clothes, houses, vehicles, and so on, it is because we have previously practised generosity or we have lavishly given the things away that we get without any difficulty now in return.

What obstructs or delays the thought of giving is greed or stinginess. It has to be overcome by giving itself. If you get into the habit of giving whatever you have, there will be nothing that you cannot give. It will enable you to easily give up anything and to be free from craving completely.

In His discourses the Supreme Buddha preaches that 'there are these two gifts, namely; material gift and the gift of Dhamma (the teachings of the supreme Buddha). Out of the two, the gift of Dhamma excels all other gifts'.

(AN 1)

Sīla (Virtue)

Sīla is the restraint of body and speech. When our body and speech are restrained, we are controlled and well behaved. When they are not restrained, we are likely to act wrongly by body and speech which will result in bad consequences in this life and the next life as well. Therefore, the quality of being virtuous is a great quality that the Supreme Buddha appreciated very much. A virtuous life makes the world beautiful and peaceful. A virtuous life makes no fear and dread to the society. Sīla is the foundation for wholesome deeds as well as meritorious deeds. All the meritorious deeds that one does, having well established in sīla, become more successful and yield great fruit and benefits.

Basically, the Buddha has imposed five precepts as sīla on lay disciples. They are: refraining from killing beings, refraining from stealing, refraining from sexual misconduct, refraining from telling lies, and refraining from taking intoxicating drinks and drugs. The Buddha preached that by observing these five precepts the noble disciple gives to an immeasurable number of beings freedom from fear, enmity and affliction. And he receives the same in return as a result. In the same discourse the Buddha taught that keeping these five precepts generates five streams of merits in the life of the person who has observed the precepts. It means the life of a person who is virtuous is filled with five streams of merits constantly.

(Puññābhisanda Sutta - AN 5)

So, the good that comes from sīla is enormous. The Buddha pointed out that there are five advantages to one who is virtuous.

1. He gains much wealth through careful attention to his affairs.

2. He gets good reputation.

3. Whatever assembly he approaches, whether it is with venerable monks, respectable people, decent, educated people, or intellectuals, he does so with confidence and assurance.

4. He dies unconfused.

5. After death he is reborn in a good destination, a heavenly world.

(Kula Sutta - AN 3)

On the other hand, if one is not virtuous, he has to experience the opposite of these advantages, that is;

1.The wealth of an unvirtuous person will be destroyed due to careless attention to his affairs.

2.An unvirtuous person cannot approach a gathering of virtuous people with courage and confidence.

3.An unvirtuous person will earn a bad reputation.

4.An unvirtuous person will die confused.

5.An unvirtuous person will be reborn in bad destinations like hell after death.

(Kula Sutta - AN 3)

Therefore, if one is afraid of suffering and likes happiness he should be well-disciplined by keeping to the five precepts. As a special benefit of sila, Supreme Buddha taught virtuous behaviour enables one to concentrate the mind easily and it is that concentration that leads to wisdom, the ability to see the things as they really are. Accordingly, sila is the foundation for all the progress and the success of the path of the Dhamma.

In reply to a question asked by a person called Jānussōni, the Supreme Buddha said that gifts such as foods, drinks, clothes, etc. given as charity without being virtuous does not yield good results. Such people who practise giving without being virtuous will be reborn among cows, elephants, horses, dogs and cats after death. As a result of generosity practised in their previous life, these animals get enough foods and drinks *(Janussoni Sutta - AN 6)*. This indicates how significant and

l it is to be virtuous so as to reap good results in future re-
hs as human and heavenly beings. Therefore, the Supreme
ldha stresses the importance of being virtuous until one's
th.

vana (Meditation)

Meditation is another way of accumulating merits.
of the three ways, mediation is the most powerful way of
erating merit. It means that meditation yields much more
it than the other two as it directly involves our mind that
ie forerunner of everything. The merit that is generated
meditation is so powerful that it can gradually lead the
litator to Nibbāna, the freedom of suffering.

Meditation is a significant aspect of Buddhism. It
bles us to see the true nature of mind by focusing on our
tered and wandering mind to get to one point which gives
he ability to see and understand the things as they really
People may meditate with different intentions but most do
have a definite goal and do not even know how to meditate.
hat respect, only Buddhism, the only realistic philosophy,
hes the real purpose of meditation and how to reach that
l. The final aim of mediation is to tame this scattered mind
l get liberated from that mind itself since it is completely
ponsible for all the sufferings we undergo. It is with this
ntion that a Buddhist should practise meditation. Thus
ditation is for purifying this mind from defilements and
this purpose, sila (virtue) is essential. That means; without
ng virtuous one is unable to gain intended results by his
ditation because the purification of mind takes place only
en the body and speech are well restrained.

A well-developed mind is one of the greatest results of meditation. A developed mind is a great blessing whereas an undeveloped mind is a danger as well as a disaster. One who has an undeveloped mind can be easily affected by lust, anger, rancour, delusion, jealousy and any other negative states of mind, and acts wrongly which finally leads to suffering. He cannot withstand the pressure and strains of life and think wisely as he is a narrow-minded person. He easily becomes a victim of stress, depression and other mental illnesses. Such a person possessing an undeveloped mind is more likely to be born in a bad destination after death. In order to get rid of such a danger, one has to develop his mind little by little in terms of a suitable subject of mediation. One with a developed mind is patient, far-sighted, mindful, and sensible. He is well-balanced in the face of gain and loss, disrepute and fame, blame and praise, and pleasure and pain.

The Buddha teaches two types of mediation:

1. Samatha meditation (Tranquillity meditation)

2. Vippassanā meditation (Insight meditation)

Samatha Meditation

The aim of Samatha meditation is concentration. Samatha means calm or tranquillity. The mind is concentrated or tranquillised when it is free from the five hindrances; namely desire for sensual pleasure, ill will, sloth and torpor, remorse and doubt. Normally our mental states are scattered in all directions because of these five hindrances. By practising a subject of Samatha meditation, you can calm your mind by temporarily subduing the five hindrances. That calmness is called 'liberation of mind (ceto vimukti)' by the Supreme Buddha.

Thus, Samatha mediation particularly helps focus your attention on one point which will result in calmness or concentration in the mind. Only when your mind is well-concentrated, you will be able to see things as they really are. Usually, it takes time for the mind to be concentrated, sometimes a month, a year, ten years, fifty years or more. It really depends on the power of your merit, dedication, perseverance, your virtue or noble human qualities and more specifically, confidence in the Triple Gem: the Supreme Buddha, Dhamma, and Sangha.

The happiness one can obtain through practising a subject of meditation is marvellous. Not to mention the happiness or bliss that one can enjoy with the ultimate result of the meditation, the bliss of Nibbāna. The Buddha teaches various subjects of Samatha meditation such as breathing meditation and loving kindness meditation. It is vital to get correct guidance from a Buddhist monk in order to obtain good results from a subject of meditation that you are going to practise.

Vipassanā Meditation

You have already learned that the aim of amatha meditation is gaining concentration by liberating the mind from five hindrances. It is not the final aim of meditaion. The mind is not liberated from defilements yet. Calmness of the mind is only a condition needed to develop insight. In other words, a calm mind is necessary to look into yourself to have a deep understanding about yourself and the world. Vpassanā meditation is carried out for that purpose.

Vipassanā gives insight into the real nature of things. Vipassanā means seeing things as they really are. When you continue to see things as they really are with a well-concentrated mind, you gain insight into impermanence, suffering and non-self. When a meditator's mind is well concentrated and he has gained mastery over that concentration then he can direct his mind to see how this life undergoes impermanence and how suffering originates because of that very impermanence. Then, he sees there is not an entity called a "self", which can control our eye, ear, nose, tongue, body and mind. When the meditator keeps on looking at these three characteristics that way, his wisdom gets matured and becomes perfected to the point that he can attain liberation fully or to some extent. That being the case, Vipassanā brings about wisdom which helps eradicate defilements from the mind. The final aim of Vipassana meditation, i.e. full freedom of suffering is called 'liberation by wisdom' *(pannavimutta)* by the Supreme Buddha.

However, concentration is not essentially required for you to practise a subject of Vipassanā meditation. You can practice it as a subject of meditation like impermanent meditation etc. But what happens there is that subject of Vipassanā meditation calms down or tranquillises the mind. When the mind is well concentrated in that Vipassanā, what is really intended by Vipassanā can then be implemented. You can practise Vipassanā or insight meditation in the level of the six bases (eye, ear, nose, tongue, body and mind) or the four elements (earth element, water element, heat element, air element) or five aggregates (form, feeling, perception, formation, consciousness) and so on.

The Supreme Buddha preached that the merit
:rated by sīla is much more than that of giving. Likewise,
merits generated by means of practising a subject of
litation is even greater than that of sīla. It does not mean
one should not give things in charity and keep precepts
that the meritorious act of meditation is sufficient. It is
lly miscomprehension, and we should make the best of
·y chance we get in order to gain merits. Particularly,
ng helps eradicate greed and stinginess, sīla helps refrain
n demerits committed by way of body and speech while
litation helps tame the mind and gain concentration.
ıs, one should put all three ways into practice as the results
y produce are different from one another.

In addition to these three ways; Dana, Sīla and
ıvana, there are many other ways of gaining merits such
·especting and taking care of parents, teachers and elderly
ɔple, giving a helping hand to others in need, building
es, ponds, reservoirs, making gardens, planting trees,
ıstructing roads, bridges, resting huts and lays-by and any
for the benefit and welfare of people as well as animals.

And with regard to Dhamma, apart from these acts
merits, listening, learning, recalling and discussing the
ıamma generate immense merits in one's life.

Therefore, the Supreme Buddha, with utmost
mpassion, preached that: " As from a great heap of flowers
ıny garlands can be made, even so, a human being should
· as many meritorious deeds as possible".

(Dhammapada - Puppha Vagga)

Anicca Bhāvanā

Impermanent Meditation ~ Six Faculties

Think in the following way and investigate with wisdom.

Since the eye is conditioned by impermanent causes, and ceases with the cessation of those causes, the eye is impermanent... impermanent... impermanent.

Since the eye is subject to change, and as I have no such power over the eye that I may say, let my eye be 'thus', let my eye not be 'thus',

the eye is not mine; I am not; not myself.

Forms are impermanent... impermanent... impermanent.

Forms are not mine; I am not; not myself.

Consciousness of eye, (which arises in dependence of eye and form), is impermanent... impermanent... impermanent.

Consciousness of eye is not mine; I am not; not myself.

Contact of eye, (the meeting of eye, form and the consciousness of eye), is impermanent... impermanent... impermanent.

Contact of eye is not mine; I am not; not myself.

Feelings - pleasant, unpleasant and neutral, (arising from the contact of eye), are impermanent... impermanent... impermanent.

Feelings are not mine; I am not; not myself.

Perception of forms, (arising from the contact of eye), is impermanent... impermanent... impermanent.

Perception of forms is not mine; not I am; not myself.

Volitions regarding forms, (arising from the contact of eye), are impermanent... impermanent... impermanent.

Volitions regarding forms are not mine; not I am; not myself.

Desire to see forms is impermanent... impermanent... impermanent.

Desire to see forms is not mine; I am not; not myself.

Since the ear is conditioned by impermanent causes, and ceases with the cessation of those causes,

the ear is impermanent... impermanent... impermanent.

Since the ear is subject to change, and as I have no such power over the ear that I may say, ,let my ear be 'thus', let my ear not be 'thus',

the ear is not mine; I am not; not myself.

Sounds are impermanent... impermanent... impermanent.

Sounds are not mine; I am not; not myself.

Consciousness of ear, (which arises in dependence of ear and sounds), is impermanent... impermanent... impermanent.

Consciousness of ear is not mine; I am not; not myself.

Contact of ear, (the meeting of ear, sound and the consciousness of ear), is impermanent... impermanent... impermanent.

Contact of ear is not mine; I am not; not myself.

Feelings, pleasant, unpleasant and neutral, (arising from the contact of ear), are impermanent... impermanent...

imperman ent.

Feelings are not mine; I am not; not myself.

Perception of sounds, (arising form the contact of ea impermanent... impermanent... impermanent.

Perception of sounds is not mine; not I am; not myself.

Volitions regarding sounds, (arising from the contact of are impermanent... impermanent... impermanent.

Volitions regarding sounds are not mine; not I am; not m

Desire to hear sounds is impermanent... impermane impermanent.

Desire to hear sounds is not mine; I am not; not myself.

Since the nose is conditioned by impermanent ca and ceases with the cessation of those causes, the no impermanent... impermanent... impermanent.

Since the nose is subject to change, and as I have no power over the nose that I may say, ,let my nose be 'thu my nose not be 'thus',

the nose is not mine; I am not; not myself.

Odours are impermanent... imperrnanent... impermane

Smells are not mine; I am not; not myself.

Consciousness of nose, (which arises in dependence of and smell), is impermanent... impermanent... imperma

Consciousness of nose is not mine; I am not; not myself.

Contact of nose, (the meeting of nose, smell and

consciousness of nose), is impermanent... impermanent... impermanent.

Contact of nose is not mine; I am not; not myself.

Feelings, pleasant, unpleasant and neutral, (arising from the contact of nose), are impermanent... impermanent... impermanent.

Feelings are not mine; I am not; not myself.

Perception of smells, (arising from the contact of nose), is impermanent... impermanent... impermanent.

Perception of smells is not mine; not I am; not myself.

Volitions regarding smells, (arising from the contact of nose) are impermanent... impermanent... impermanent.

Volitions regarding smells are not mine; not I am; not myself

Desire to smell odours is impermanent... impermanent.. impermanent.

Desire to smell odours is not mine; I am not; not myself.

Since the tongue is conditioned by impermanent causes and ceases with the cessation of those causes, the tongue is impermanent... impermanent... impermanent.

Since the tongue is subject to change, and as I have no such power over the tongue that I may say, ,let my tongue be 'thus let my tongue not be 'thus,

the tongue is not mine; I am not; not myself.

Tastes are impermanent... impermanent... impermanent.

Tastes are not mine; I am not; not myself.

Consciousness of tongue, (which arises in dependence of tongue and taste), is impermanent... impermanent... impermanent.

Consciousness of tongue is not mine; I am not; not myself.

Contact of tongue, (the meeting of tongue, tastes and the consciousness of tongue),

is impermanent... impermanent... impermanent.

Contact of tongue is not mine; I am not; not myself.

Feelings, pleasant, unpleasant and neutral, (arising from the contact of tongue), are impermanent... impermanent... impermanent.

Feelings are not mine; I am not; not myself.

Perception of tastes, (arising from the contact of tongue), is impermanent... impermanent... impermanent.

Perception of tastes is not mine; not I am; not myself.

Volitions regarding tastes, (arising from the contact of tongue), are impermanent... impermanent... impermanent.

Volitions regarding tastes are not mine; not I am; not myself.

The desire to taste is impermanent... impermanent... impermanent.

Desire to taste is not mine; I am not; not myself.

Since the body is conditioned by impermanent causes, and ceases with the cessation of those causes, the body is impermanent... impermanent... impermanent.

Since the body is subject to change, and as I have no such power over the body that I may say, ,let my body be 'thus', let my body not be 'thus,

the body is not mine; I am not; not myself.

Tangibles are impermanent... impermanent... impermanent.

Tangibles are not mine; I am not; not myself.

Consciousness of body, (which arises in dependence of body and tangibles), is impermanent... impermanent... impermanent.

Consciousness of body is not mine; I am not; not myself.

Contact of body, (the meeting of body, tangibles and the consciousness of body), is impermanent... impermanent... impermanent.

Contact of body is not mine; I am not; not myself.

Feelings, pleasant, unpleasant and neutral, (arising from the contact of body), are impermanent... impermanent... impermanent.

Feelings are not mine; I am not; not myself.

Perception of tangibles, (arising from the contact of body), is impermanent... impermanent... impermanent.

Perception of tangibles is not mine; not I am; not myself.

Volitions regarding tangibles, (arising from the contact of body), are impermanent... impermanent... impermanent.

Volitions regarding tangibles are not mine; not I am; not myself.

The desire for tangibles is impermanent... impermanent... impermanent.

Desire for tangibles is not mine; I am not; not myself.

Since the mind is conditioned by impermanent causes, and ceases with the cessation of those causes, the mind is impermanent... impermanent... impermanent.

Since the mind is subject to change, and as I have no such power over the mind that I may say, ,let my mind be 'thus', let my mind not be 'thus,

the mind is not mine; I am not; not myself.

Thoughts are impermanent... impermanent... impermanent.

Thoughts are not mine; I am not; not myself.

Consciousness of mind, (which arises in dependence of mind and thoughts), is impermanent... impermanent... impermanent.

Consciousness of mind is not mine; I am not; not myself.

Contact of mind, (the meeting of mind, thoughts and the consciousness of mind), is impermanent... impermanent... impermanent.

Contact of mind is not mine; I am not; not myself.

Feelings, pleasant, unpleasant and neutral, (arising from the contact of mind), are impermanent... impermanent... impermanent.

Feelings are not mine; I am not; not myself.

Perception of thoughts, (arising from the contact of mind), is impermanent... impermanent... impermanent.

Perception of thoughts is not mine; not I am; not myself.

Volitions regarding thought, (arising from the contact of mind), impermanent... impermanent... impermanent.

Volitions regarding thoughts are not mine; not I am; not myself.

The desire for thoughts is impermanent... impermanent... impermanent.

Desire for thoughts is not mine; I am not; not myself.

Sādhu! Sādhu! Sādhu!

Chapter Eight

The man who performs meritorious deeds is happy in this world and the next. He is happy in both worlds. He feels happy at the thought: 'I have done merits. It will be happier when born in a heavenly world'.

- Dhammapada -

The Heavenly Worlds

There are six heavenly worlds mentioned by the Buddha. They are situated above the human world. Those worlds and the heavenly beings cannot be seen with our naked eyes or any other modern instrument because those worlds and their inhabitants are not made up of material things. Heavenly beings enjoy much more happiness than us, the human beings. The Buddha said even the happiness enjoyed by a Wheel-turning Monarch who rules the whole world is very little when compared to the happiness of a heavenly being.

Who is a Wheel – turning Monarch ?

A Wheel – turning Monarch is a king who is endowed with the seven treasures and the four properties. Because of that he experiences incredible happiness. What are the seven? Once, on a full-moon day, when the King has washed his head and gone up to the verandah on top of his palace, the divine Wheel-treasure appears to him, thousand-spoked, complete with felloe, hub and all appurtenances. On seeing it, the King thinks: "I have heard that when a duly anointed Khattiya king sees such a wheel, he will become a wheel-turning monarch. May I become such a monarch!"

Then, rising from his seat, covering one shoulder with his robe, the King took a gold vessel in his left hand, sprinkled the Wheel with his right hand, and says: "May the noble Wheel-Treasure turn, may the noble Wheel-Treasure conquer!" The Wheel turns to the east, and King follows it with his fourfold army(Elephant,cavalry,chariots and infantry).

And in whatever country the Wheel stops, the King takes up residence with his fourfold army.

And those kings who face him in the eastern region come and say: "Come, Your Majesty, welcome! We are yours, Your Majesty. Rule us, Your Majesty!" And the King says: "Do not take life. Do not take what is not given. Do not commit sexual misconduct. Do not tell lies. Do not take intoxicating drinks and drugs. And those who have faced him in the eastern region became his subjects.

And when the Wheel has plunged into the eastern sea, it emerges and turns south, and King follows it with his fourfold army. And those Kings..., become his subjects. Having plunged into the southern sea it turns west..., having plunged into the western sea it turns north,and King follows it with his fourfold army and those who have faced him in the northern region become his subjects.

Then the Wheel-Treasure, having conquered the lands from sea to sea, returns to the royal capital and stops before the King's palace as if to adorn the royal palace. And this is how the Wheel-Treasure appears to the King.

Then the Elephant-Treasure appears to the King, pure of sevenfold strength, with the wonderful power of travelling through the air, a royal tusker called Uposatha. Seeing him, the King thinks: "What a wonderful riding-elephant, if only he could be brought under control!" And this Elephant-Treasure submits to control just like a thoroughbred that has been trained for a long time. And once the King, to try him, mounts the Elephant-Treasure at crack of dawn and rides him from sea to sea, returning to the city in time for breakfast. And that is how the Elephant-Treasure appears to the King.

Then the Horse-Treasure appears to the King, with a crow's dark-maned, with the wondrous power of travelling through the air, a royal stallion called. Valāhaka and the King thinks: 'What a wonderful mount, if only he could be brought under control!" And this Horse-Treasure submits to control just like a thoroughbred that has been trained for a long time... And that is how the Horse-Treasure appears to the King.

Then the Jewel-Treasure appears to the King. It is a beryl, pure, excellent, well-cut into eight facets, clear, bright, unflawed, perfect in every respect. The lustre of this Jewel-Treasure radiates for an entire yōjana (ten kilometres) round about. And once the King, to try it, goes on a thick dark night with his four-fold army, with the Jewel-Treasure fixed to the top of his flag. And all who live in the villages round about starts their daily work, thinking it is daylight. And that is how the Jewel-Treasure appears to the King.

Then the Woman-Treasure appears to King, lovely, fair to see, charming, with a lotus-like complexion, not too tall or too short, not too thin or too fat, not too dark or too fair, of more than human, deva-like beauty. And the touch of the skin of the Woman-Treasure was like cotton or silk, and her limbs were cool when it is hot, and warm when it is cold. Her body smells of sandal-wood and her lips of lotus. This Woman-Treasure rises before the King and retires later, and is always willing to do his pleasure, and she was pleasant of speech. And this Woman-Treasure is not unfaithful to the King even in thought, much less in deed. And that is how the Woman-Treasure appears to the King.

Then the Householder-Treasure appears to the King. With the divine eye which, as the result of kamma, he sees where treasure, owned and ownerless, is hidden. He comes to the King and says: "Have no fear, Your Majesty, I will look after your wealth properly." And once, the King, to try him, goes on board a ship and has it taken to the current in the middle of the Ganges. Then he says to the Householder-Treasure: "Householder, I want some gold coin!" 'Well then, Sire, let the ship be brought to one bank." "I want the gold coins here!" Then the householder touches the water with both hands and draws out a vessel full of gold coins, saying: "Is that enough, Sire? Will that do, Sire?" and the King says: "That is enough, householder, that will do, you have served me enough." And that is how the Householder-Treasurer appears to the King.

Then the Counsellor-Treasure appears to the King. He is wise, experienced, clever and competent to advise the King on how to proceed with what should be proceeded with, and to withdraw from what should be withdrawn from, and to overlook what should be overlooked. He comes to the King and says: "Have no fear, Your Majesty, I shall advise you." And that is how the Counsellor-Treasure appears to the King and how he is equipped with all the seven treasures.

The King is endowed with the four properties. Firstly, the

King is handsome, good to look at, pleasing, with a complexion like the finest lotus, surpassing other men. Secondly, he is long-lived, outliving other men. Thirdly, he is free from illness, free from sickness, with a healthy digestion, less subject to cold and heat than that of other men. Fourthly, he is beloved and popular with Brahmins and householders. Just as a father is beloved by his children, so he is with Brahmins and householders. And they are beloved by the King as children are beloved by their father. Once the King sets out for the pleasure-park with his fourfold army, and the Brahmins and householders come to him and say: "Pass slowly by, Sire, that we may see you as long as possible!" And the King said to the charioteer: "Drive the chariot slowly so that I can see these Brahmins and householders as long as possible."

(Balapandita Sutta - MN 3)

Thus, the King is endowed with these four properties and he is the most fortunate human being on the earth because of his previously accumulated enormous merits. But the Supreme Buddha said that the great happiness the Wheel-Turning Monarch enjoys is so little that it is similar to that of a beggar when compared with the happiness experienced by a heavenly being.

The life span of the heavenly beings is also longer than ours. Heavenly worlds are for those who refrain from doing demerits and do merits by body, speech and mind.

It is not easy to be born in a heavenly world. The Supreme Buddha preached that only a very few people are reborn in heavenly worlds after death. Rebirth in to a heavenly world cannot be gained by mere words, prayers or a wish.

One should follow the path leading to the heavenly world. That path is none other than the accumulation of merits. In other words, human beings who cultivate good human qualities and spiritual values in themselves are bound to take rebirth in heavenly worlds. In order to perform meritorious acts and develop moral human qualities, one should be basically of Mundane Right View.* Apart from that, in an age where a Buddha appears, the easiest way to heavenly worlds is going to the Buddha, Dhamma and Sangha for refuge.

The Supreme Buddha emphasised that if one goes to the Buddha for refuge, with understanding of him, the person will not be born in a bad destination but among heavenly beings after death. In addition, the Supreme Buddha preached that one who develops five qualities in him, is destined to be reborn in a heavenly world.

They are;

1) Confidence – (Shraddhā)
He develops his confidence in the Buddha, Dhamma and Sangha in such a way that it can never be shaken.

2) Virtue – (Sīla)
The restraint of body and speech.

3) Knowledge of Dhamma – (Suta)
He listens to the teachings of the Buddha, learns them by heart and is armed with good knowledge of Dhamma.

---

*Described in Chapter 6

4) Generosity – (Chāga)

He practises giving food, drinks, clothes etc. lavishly to the Sangha; the incomparable field of merit, and to those in need. He practises giving in such a way that the stinginess and greed dormant in the mind are abandoned.

5) Wisdom – (Pañña)

He develops wisdom by way of wisely reflecting on the Dhamma he heard and hears, and practising meditation.

The supreme Buddha, the Knower of the world saw the heavenly worlds with His divine eye and disclosed all facts about them with utmost compassion. Given below are the six heavenly worlds and the details taught by the Blessed One.

1. Chāthummaharājika

Deities who live in the heavenly world Chāthummaharājika are ruled by the Four Great Kings - Dhataratta, Virūdha, Virūpakkha, Vessawana. A single day and night is equivalent to fifty human years; thirty such days make up a month and twelve such months make up a year. The life span of those Deities is five hundred such celestial years.

2. Thāvatimsa

A single night and day is equivalent to hundred human years for deities residing in Thāvatimsa. Thirty such days make up a month and twelve such months make up a year. The life span of those deities is one thousand such celestial years.

3. Yāma

A single night and day is equivalent to two hundred human years for Yāma deities. Thirty such days make up a month and twelve such months make up a year. The life span of those deities is two thousand such celestial years.

4. Thusita

A single night and day is equivalent to four hundred human years for Thusita deities. Thirty such days make up a month and twelve such months make up a year. The life span of those deities is four thousand such celestial years.

5. Nimmānarathi – Deities who rejoice in creation

A single night and day is equivalent to eight hundred human years for deities who live in Nimmānarathi. Thirty such days make up a month and twelve such months make up a year. The life span of those deities is eight thousand such celestial years. The Nimmānarathi deities create happiness for themselves just when they think of it.

6. Paranimmitha asavatthi

A single night and day is equivalent to sixteen hundred human years for Paranimmitha Vasavatthi deities. Thirty such days make up a month and twelve such months make up a year. The life span of deities is sixteen thousand such celestial years.

(Visakha Uposatha Sutta - AN 5)

There is much more protection in heavenly worlds than in the human world. Human qualities are speedily deteriorating. People are losing their values and ethics, once highly esteemed above everything else. The moral values are not respected and they have gone to dogs. Amidst the world's temptation, people are blinded by sensual pleasures. Terrorism is likely to rein the world.

The Supreme Buddha who foresaw the future of the world proclaimed that due to the deterioration of ethics of mankind, a time will come when people will have a life-span of ten years. And with them, girls will be marriageable at the age of five years. And with them, these flavours will disappear: ghee, butter, sesame-oil, treacle and salt. Among the foods Kudrūsa-grain[1] will be the chief food, just as rice and curry are today. And with them, the ten courses of moral conduct[2] will completely disappear, and the ten courses of evil[3] will prevail exceedingly; for those of a ten-year life span there will be no word "wholesome", so how can there be anyone who acts in a moral way? Those people who have no respect for mother or father, for ascetics and Brahmins, for the head of the family, will be the ones who enjoy honour and prestige. Just as it is now the people who show respect for mother and father, for ascetics and Brahmins, for the head of the family, who are praised and honoured, so it will be with those who do the opposite.

Among those of a ten-year life-span, no account will be taken of mother or aunt, of mother's sister-in-law, of teacher's wife or of one's father's wives and so on - all will be immoral in the world, like goats and sheep, fowl and pigs, dogs and jackals. Among them, fierce enmity will prevail for one another; fierce hatred, fierce anger and thoughts of

---

[1] A type of grain which is coarse and tasteless

[2] Abstaining from killings beings, abstaining from stealing, abstaining from sexual misconduct, abstaining from telling lies, abstaining from divisive speech, abstaining from harsh speech, abstaining from idle chatter, abstaining from hate, abstaining from greed and abstaining from Wrong View.

[3] The opposite of the ten courses of moral conduct

killing, mother against child and child against mother, father against child and child against father, brother against brother, brother against sister; just as the hunter feels hatred for the beast he stalks.

And for those of a ten-year life-span, there will come to be a 'sword- interval' of seven days, during which they will mistake one another for wild beasts. Sharp swords will appear in their hands and evil thoughts will occur: "There is a wild beast! Let's destroy them!" With these thoughts, they will take each other's lives with those swords.

(Cakkavatti Seehanada Sutta - DN 3)

Therefore, it is advisable to restrain the mind, body and speech, while performing meritorious acts and developing good human qualities like loving-kindness, patience, humility, generosity etc. so as to be reborn in a heavenly world, the only secured place until Nibbāna is realized.

Chapter Nine

One is defiled by one's own evil. One is purified by refraining from evil. Purity and impurity depend on oneself. No one can purify another.

- *Dhammapada* -

Bad Destinations

Bad destinations are lower worlds which are full of suffering. Those who commit sinful deeds and do not live by the teachings of the Buddha are reborn in these bad worlds. The life span of the beings born in these worlds is very long. It is measured by way of aeons.

What is an aeon?

It is not easy to count an aeon and say it is so many years or so many hundreds of years, or so many thousands of years, or so many hundreds of thousands of years.

The Supreme Buddha gave a simile for us to understand the length of an aeon.

The Buddha said "suppose, bhikku, there was a city with iron walls ten kilometres long, ten kilometres wide and ten kilometres high, filled with mustard seeds as dense as a topknot. At the end of every hundred years a man would remove one mustard seed from there. The great heap of mustard seeds might by this effort be eliminated but the aeon would still not have come to an end".

(Sasapa Sutta - SN 2)

The four bad destinations are hell, the ghost world, the asura world, and the animal world. Why do beings take rebirth in these bad realms? Rebirth in these worlds of course does not take place according to a god's or someone else's order or a wish. Beings themselves are responsible for rebirth in these places of misery. One's own bad kamma by thoughts, words, and deeds leads to these lower worlds. According to the teachings of the Supreme Buddha, it is the four bad destinations that are the most frequented by beings. It is just like the house one lives in. Wherever one goes, he returns home. Similarly, a being rarely gets an opportunity to be born in the human world or in a heavenly world but returns to a bad realm more frequently due to the bad kamma committed by him. It is because in the lower realms no opportunity exists to perform meritorious deeds. Animals, for example, have to struggle for existence, preying upon each other. Whatever the beings in lower realms do, speak, and think are prone to produce a bad outcome again.

Given below are some discourses delivered by the Supreme Buddha to point out the danger that exists for the beings born there.

Passing away from Hell (Niraya Chuti Suttas)

The Blessed One took up a little bit of soil in his finger nail and addressed the bhikkus thus,

"What do you think, bhikkus, which is more: the little bit of soil on my finger nail or the great earth?"

"Venerable Sir, the great earth is more. The little bit of soil that the Blessed One has taken up on his fingernail is trifling. Compared to the great earth, the little bit of soil that the Blessed One has taken up on his finger nail is not calculable, does not bear comparison, does not amount even to a fraction. So too, bhikkus, those beings are few who, when they pass away from hell, are reborn among human beings "

"But those beings are numerous who, when they pass away from hell, are reborn in hell...in the animal realm...in the domain of ghosts..."

Passing Away from Hell

"...So too, bhikkus, those beings are few who, when they pass away from hell, are reborn among devas. But those beings are more numerous who, when they pass away from hell, are reborn in hell...in the animal realm...in the domain of ghosts..."

(Nirayacuti Sutta - SN 5)

Passing Away from the Animal Realm

"...So too, bhikkus, those beings are few who, when they pass away from the animal realm, are reborn among human beings. But those beings are more numerous who, when they pass away from the animal realm, are reborn in hell...in the animal realm...in the domain of ghosts..."

Passing Away from the Animal Realm

"...So too, bhikkus, those beings are few who, when they pass away from the animal realm, are reborn among devas. But those beings are more numerous who, when they pass away from the animal realm, are reborn in hell...in the animal realm...in the domain of ghosts..."

(Tiraccanacuti Sutta - SN 5)

Passing Away from the Domain of Ghosts

"...So too, bhikkus, those beings are few who, when they pass away from the domain of ghosts, are reborn among human beings. But those beings are more numerous who, when they pass away from the domain of ghosts, are reborn in hell...in the animal realm...in the domain of ghosts...

Passing Away from the Domain of Ghosts

"...So too, bhikkus, those beings are few who, when they pass away from the domain of ghosts, are reborn among devas. But those beings are more numerous who, when they pass away from the domain of ghosts, are reborn in hell...in the animal realm...in the domain of ghosts..."

(Petacuti Sutta - SN 5)

These discourses show us how dangerous it is to be reborn in bad destinations. In the present materialised world, most of the people blinded by sensual pleasures and modern technology do not believe that there are lower realms like these. They will come to know it for themselves, once they fall into one of these lower realms. Therefore, it is advisable to refrain in advance from the actions which lead to these worlds as those who like happiness and detest suffering.

Specially, the Supreme Buddha at the end of the above sermons shows us that beings are reborn in such lower worlds because they have not seen the Four Noble Truths, namely Suffering , the Origin of Suffering, the Cessation of Suffering and the way leading to the Cessation of Suffering and therefore stressed the importance of realising them with utmost effort.

Chapter Ten

Of all paths the Noble Eightfold Path is the best; of all truths the Four Noble Truths are the best; of all things passionless Nibbāna is the best; Of humans, the Buddha is the best.

- Dhammapada -

The Four Noble Truths

A Buddha appears in the world in order to make fortunate beings -gods and humans- understand the Four Noble Truths. When one fully understands the Four Noble Truths, he gets the freedom from all the sufferings he has to undergo. If one fails to understand them, then he has to experience infinite and untold suffering by being born again and again in various existences including the four bad destinations.

The Four Noble Truths are the central teaching of Buddhism. Almost all the sermons delivered by the Buddha are aimed at realising the Four Noble Truths. A truth is something that never changes and is common to all regardless of caste, creed, sex, religion, age and complexion.

What are the Four Noble Truths?

1. The Noble Truth of Suffering

The Buddha describes this truth this way: 'Birth is suffering, ageing is suffering, sickness is suffering, death is suffering, association with disagreeable people and unpleasant things is suffering, separation from loved ones and pleasant things is suffering, not receiving what one desires is suffering. In brief, the five aggregates of clinging are suffering'. Any type of suffering one undergoes comes under one of these forms and therefore no one can add something different to the things in this list. Our whole life is inseparably tied up with suffering-dukka in Pali. It erupts into the open as unsatisfactoriness, despair, grief, disappointment, sorrow, anger, fear, pain,

loneliness, insecurity, frustration and so on. No one is exempt
from suffering other than the Enlightened Ones. Everyone
suffers from birth to death. It is true that there are pleasures as
well in our life, but they are only momentary. They only make
us happy as long as they last. They never last forever. They
must come to an end leaving us feeling deprived. At the end of
happiness there is suffering (dukka). Things are never perfect
or meet our expectation. There is always a vacuum in our
life which can never be filled. Beings, except for Enlightened
Ones (arahants), never die peacefully but unsatisfactorily. As
a result of their delusion, beings do not understand that there
is suffering in life. Instead, they only chase after something
agreeable and pleasant to overcome the present suffering, but
they are never satisfied with anything.

The Buddha appears in the world in order to teach this
reality. Almost all His sermons (suttas) enlighten us with the
fact that there is suffering in everything and in every existence.
In particular, He teaches vividly how suffering is originated,
that is, from craving.

2. The Noble Truth of the Origin of Suffering

It is the craving which produces re-existence,
accompanied by passionate lust and finding delight now here
and now there, namely, craving for sense-pleasures, craving for
existence and craving for nonexistence. Craving is the origin
or root cause of suffering. The Supreme Buddha preached
that wherever in the world there is anything agreeable and
pleasurable, there this craving arises and establishes itself. It
is a wonderful discovery that suffering springs from craving

or desire. The more agreeable and pleasurable things one has craving for, the more suffering that one has to experience. The less agreeable and pleasurable things one has, the less suffering that he has to experience. In this way, if there is nothing agreeable and pleasurable which beings develop craving for, there is no suffering to be experienced.

The Supreme Buddha mentioned that this craving which causes suffering is a fetter. He said "I do not see any single fetter other than the fetter of craving by which beings are so tied with and for so long a time run on and wander in samsara. Just as a little tree, though cut down, sprouts up again if its roots remain uncut and firm, even so, until the craving that lies dormant in the mind is rooted out, suffering springs up again and again (Dhammapada). Therefore, no one can put an end to suffering and escape from the round of rebirths (samsara) as long as craving, the maker of suffering, is completely eliminated. The Supreme Buddha's appearance is to help both human and heavenly beings eradicate this craving and attain Nibbāna, that is the cessation of that very craving.

3. The Noble Truth of the End of Suffering

It is the complete cessation of that very craving. That is what we call 'Nibbāna'.

What is Nibbāna?

The Supreme Buddha describes Nibbāna as the highest bliss, as the supreme state of sublime peace. This is the ultimate goal of the Noble Eightfold Path. Nibbāna is the end result of the destruction of lust, hatred and delusion. Where there is no lust (rāga), hatred (dōsa) and delusion (mōha), there is that supreme bliss. And also, where there is no craving, there is the end of suffering, the supreme bliss of Nibbāna. There is no birth, ageing, illness and death in Nibbāna. Hence, the Supreme Buddha preaches that Nibbāna is "the unborn, unageing, unailing, deathless, sorrowless, undefiled supreme security from bondage."

(Nibbana Sutta - KN 1)

Nibbāna is irreversible and not subject to change. It is eternal. In Buddhism, the term 'unconditioned' is used to describe Nibbāna. Three characteristics are seen in a conditioned thing. They are: arising, ceasing and changing while existing. These three characteristics are not seen in Nibbāna. Furthermore, Nibbāna is devoid of 'cause and effect' (Dependent Origination). The Supreme Buddha points out the Noble Eightfold Path as the key to Nibbāna.

4.The Noble Truth of the Path Leading to the End of Suffering

It is just this Noble Eightfold Path, namely: right view, right intention, right speech, right action, right livelihood, right effort, right mindfulness and right concentration.

The Noble Eightfold Path is the direct and one and only way to end suffering. There is no other clear-cut way leading to the end of suffering anywhere in this universe. Whether humans or gods, everyone who wishes to make an end of suffering should follow this path. 'Sōtha' is another term for the Noble Eightfold Path which means 'stream' in the sense that just as a stream directly flows towards the ocean, the person who follows this noble path goes straight in the direction of Nibbāna, freedom of suffering. The Noble Eightfold Path is also known as 'Middle Way'. It is the middle way because it keeps away from two extremes, two misguided attempts to gain release from suffering. One is the extreme of indulgence in sense pleasure and the other is the practice of self-mortification, the attempt to gain liberation by afflicting the body.

What is special about this path is that one who follows this path as taught by the Buddha will definitely succeed one day or another. The Supreme Buddha having first discovered this path attained the supreme bliss of Nibbāna. Then He disclosed that path to beings in the world in order for them to follow it and attain Nibbāna because He knows that this path has the capacity to lead us to the full and final end of suffering.

The Supreme Buddha himself describes the middle way, the Noble Eightfold Path as the way that gives rise to vision, gives rise to knowledge, and leads to peace, to direct knowledge, to Enlightenment, to Nibbāna.

The Noble Eightfold Path consists of eight factors. They are divided into three groups or aggregates. They are the aggregate of virtue or moral discipline (Sīla), the aggregate of concentration (Samādhi) and the aggregate of Wisdom (Pañña). Right speech, right action and right livelihood make up the aggregate of Sīla; right effort, right mindfulness and right concentration make up the aggregate of Samādhi; right view and right intention make up the aggregate of pañña. Accordingly, the path is three fold training and the path factors are arranged according to a sequence. The path evolves through these three stages with Sīla or moral discipline as the foundation for concentration, concentration as the foundation for wisdom. However, it is apparent that wisdom which includes right view and right intention is the last stage of the three fold training, but its factors are placed at the beginning rather than at its end. It is precisely because one without a clear understanding about the main issue, suffering which is the right view will never want to follow the path. Only when he is aware of the problem of suffering, he places the trust in the effectiveness of the path and follows it with the intention of getting rid of suffering.

The Noble Eightfold Path is the greatest discovery ever in the world which enables us to bring suffering to an end. Explaining the greatness of the Noble Eightfold Path, the Supreme Buddha said "To whatever extent there are phenomena that are conditioned, the Noble Eightfold Path is declared the foremost among them. Those who have confidence in the Noble Eightfold Path have confidence in the foremost and for those who have confidence in the foremost, the result is foremost."

(Aggappasada Sutta - AN 2)

The Noble Eight fold Path.

1. Sammā Ditti (Right View)

That is; the knowledge of suffering, the knowledge of the origin of suffering, the knowledge of the cessation of suffering and the knowledge of the way leading to the cessation of suffering.

2. Sammā Sankappa (Right Intention)

That is; the intention of renunciation, intention of non-ill will, and the intention of non-harming.

3. Sammā Vācha (Right Speech)

That is; refraining from false speech, refraining from divisive speech, refraining from harsh speech and refraining from pointless talk.

4. Sammā Kammanta (Right Action)

That is; refraining from killing beings, refraining from stealing and refraining from sexual misconduct.

5. Sammā Ājivo (Right Livelihood)

Here, a noble disciple, having abandoned wrong livelihood, earns his living by right livelihood.

6. Sammā Vāyāmo (Right Effort)

That is; to prevent the arising of unarisen unwholesome states; to abandon unwholesome states that have already arisen; to generate wholesome states that have not yet arisen; to maintain and perfect wholesome states already arisen.

7. Sammā Sati (Right Mindfulness)

That is; Contemplation of body as body; Contemplation of feeling as feeling; Contemplation of mind as mind; Contemplation of mind-objects as mind-objects.

8. Sammā Samādhi (Right Concentration)

That is; the first Jhana, the second Jhana, the third Jhana and the fourth Jhana.

The lives of all living beings are covered by thick darkness as far as the Four Noble Truths are not realised and taught to the world by a Buddha. Until then, beings are born in darkness, age in darkness and die in darkness. Because of not understanding the Four Noble Truths, they take rebirth in lower worlds again and again and experience immense suffering. Therefore, the only solution to this great mass of suffering is to realise the Four Noble Truths.

In order to highlight the greater importance of realising the Four Noble Truths, the Supreme Buddha said "Bhikkus there were a man with a life span of a hundred years, who could live a hundred years. Someone would say to him: "come good man, in the morning you will be struck with a hundred spears; at noon you will be struck with a hundred spears; in the evening you will be struck with a hundred spears. And you good man, being struck day after day by three hundred spears will have a life span of a hundred years, will live a hundred years; and then after a hundred years you will realise the Four Noble Truths that you had not realised before".

The Supreme Buddha said: "it is fitting for a man to accept the offer who sees the value of realising the Truths. For what reason? Because this Samsara is without discoverable beginning; a starting point is not seen of times of being struck by spears, swards and axes. Even though this may be so, bhikkus, I do not say that realising the Four Noble Truths is accompanied by suffering or displeasure, but I say that the Four Noble Truths should be realised with happiness and joy".

(Balapandita Sutta - SN 5)

This sermon clearly indicates how seriously we should take the danger of not understanding the Four Noble Truths into consideration.

Only does a Buddha know the suffering one has to undergo if one is unable to realise the Four Noble Truths. Therefore, He often said to the disciples that they should make a determined effort to understand the Four Noble Truths. When we consider the suffering experienced and suffering to be experienced, our top priority should be, therefore, given to realise the Four Noble Truths above everything else. It is such a priority that the Supreme Buddha said if one's clothes and head were ablaze, he, without paying attention to them, should arouse extraordinary desire, make an extraordinary effort and exercise mindfulness and clear comprehension to realise the Four Noble Truths as they really are.

Chapter Eleven

In whatever Dhamma and discipline the Noble Eightfold Path is not found, the first ascetic (stream-enterer) is not found, the second (once-returner) the third (non-returner) or the fourth (the Arahant).

- *Maha PariNibbāna Sutta* -

Attainments of Enlightenment

The Supreme Buddha's teachings is not something based on any scriptures or someone else's view, but it is the reality of life that He realized on his own. There is a gradual process in his teachings. It starts with confidence (Shraddha) in the Buddha, His teachings, and His enlightened disciples, and ends with the result of Nibbāna (Freedom from suffering). The path leading to Nibbāna is the Noble Eightfold Path. Not all who follow this path realise the ultimate goal at once. Those who have well-developed wisdom would do so as in the Buddha's time. Others who do not have adequate wisdom have to reach the ultimate goal step by step achieving other attainments on the path. All in all, there are four attainments of enlightenment. They are: the fruit of stream-entry, the fruit of once-returning, the fruit of non-returning and the fruit of Arahantship. These four stages are described here in terms of a tenfold group called ten fetters (Samyojana) which have tied the beings firmly to the round of rebirths (Samsara).

Ten Fetters

1. *Identity view (Sakkāya Ditti):*

That is the deeply-rooted view of a self in one's life. Beings because of delusion mistakenly believe that there is a self in themselves as 'I am', 'mine' and 'myself' and that it wanders on from life to life. If there was a self, it should be able to control or stop being ill, getting old, dying, being born in miserable worlds and all the suffering beings undergo. But there is only a result of a cause as pointed out by the supreme Buddha.

The Buddha teaches these five aggregates affected by clinging are called Identity View; that is, the material form aggregate affected by clinging, the feeling aggregate affected by clinging, the perception aggregate affected by clinging, the formations aggregate affected by clinging and the consciousness aggregate affected by clinging.

2. Doubt (Vichikichcha):

That is the doubt about the Buddha, His teachings, His enlightened disciples, Virtue (Síla), Concentration (Samādhi), Wisdom (Pańńa), Liberation (Nibbāna).

3. Adherence to external rules and observances (Sílabbata parāmāsa):

That is to follow wrong ritualistic or ascetic practices in the belief that they can bring purification or liberation from suffering. For example, there are those who sink in very cold water in the morning, refuse clothes and remain naked, sleep on thorny mats and heated rocks, live like cows and dogs and many other wrong practices.

4. Sensual desire (Kamarāga):

That is the desire for forms, sounds, smells, tastes and bodily contacts.

5. Ill will (Patigha): That is anger, hate, aversion.

6. Desire for rebirth in the form-sphere of existence (Rūpa rāga):

That is desire for being born in Brahma world where beings have subtle kind of form (body).

7. *Desire for rebirth in the formless-sphere of existence (Arūpa rāga):*

That is desire for being born in the Brahma world situated above the form-realm mentioned above. These Brahmas' form (Body) is extremely subtle because of jhanas (meditative absorption) they developed.

8. *Conceit (Māna):* That is self-regard pride.

9. *Restlessness (Uddachcha)*

10. *Ignorance (Avijja):*

That is not knowing the Noble Truth of suffering, the Noble Truth of the origin of suffering, the Noble Truth of the end of suffering, and the Noble Truth of the way leading to the end of suffering.

The first five fetters are known as the lower fetters and the next as the higher fetters.

The Four Attainments of Enlightenment

The Fruit of Stream-entry.

This is the first attainment the disciple obtains by following the path. As a result of following the path the disciple eradicates the first three fetters, namely identity view, doubt and adherence to external rules and observances. It is these three fetters that drag beings down to bad destinations like hell. When the disciple realises the fruit of the path, he becomes a stream enterer. He will never be reborn in bad destinations. He has entered the 'Stream', the Noble Eightfold Path that leads the disciple irreversibly towards the Nibbāna. Now he is able to complete the path and attain Nibbāna even without a support from another. He will reach the ultimate goal, Nibbāna, in a maximum of seven births which all occur either in the human world or in heavenly worlds.

The Supreme Buddha at one time taking some soil on His fingernail preached that the suffering the noble disciple, 'the stream-enterer' has eradicated is similar to the soil in the great earth and the suffering he has yet to experience is so little that it is similar to the soil on His fingernail. This indicates what a precious thing it is to become a stream enterer that marks the end of a considerable mass of suffering in one's life. It is such a great victory to win the fruit of stream-entry that Supreme Budhda said "The fruition of stream-entry is better than sole sovereignty over the earth, going to heaven and lordship over all the worlds."

The Fruit of Once-Returning

The noble disciple who has reaped the fruit of stream-entry follows the path further to obtain the next attainment, once-returning. As a result, the path weakens the gravity of the root defilements of lust, hatred, and delusion. He becomes a Once-returner (Sakadāgāmi) as soon as he realises the fruit of the path. He is due to return either to the human world or to a heavenly world only once and there he attains the Arahanship making the end of suffering forever.

The Fruit of Non- Returning

The noble disciple becomes a non-returner (anāgāmi) as the path he follows eradicates the next two fetters, sensual desire and ill-will. The Anāgāmi disciple is bound to attain the final goal of Nibbāna after taking spontaneous rebirth in one of the five special Brahma worlds called the 'Pure Abodes' (Sudhdhāvāsa) without ever returning from that world to the human world and the six heavenly worlds.

The Fruit of Arahantship

The final attainment that is the ultimate goal of any disciple who follows the Dhamma is Arahantship, the complete destruction of defilements by following the path. The noble disciple gets rid of higher fetters: desire for rebirth in the form realm, desire for rebirth in the formless realm, conceit, restlessness and ignorance. Once realising the fruit of the path, he becomes an Arahant, putting an end to the round of rebirth. The Supreme Buddha in various suttas described the Arahant thus: he is "one with taints destroyed, who has lived a holy life, done what had to be done, laid down the burden, reached his own goal, destroyed the fetters of being and is completely liberated through final knowledge."

Arahants are no longer subject to return to any realm of existence, whether sense-sphere existence, form-sphere existence or formless-sphere existence. They have destroyed old Kamma. The mind of an Arahant is not touched by gain and loss, dispute and fame, blame and praise and pleasure and pain. They are as firm as a high pillar and as pure as a deep pool free from mud. Their thoughts, speech, and deeds are all calm. They do not cling to anything just as a dew drop that slips down the lotus leaf. They illuminate the world like the moon freed from a cloud. The Arahants, the fully liberated ones fade out just as a lamp does.

Chapter Twelve

So, if you are scared of suffering and disgusted by suffering,
then never commit evil kamma either in public or in private.

- *Kumāraka Sutta* -

What is Kamma?

It is only through Buddhism that we get wider awareness of kamma. The Supreme Buddha fully realised kamma and therefore he had the perfect knowledge about kamma, the nature of kamma, how it originates, how it works and how one can escape from it.

The word kamma literally means action. That is; bodily action, verbal action and mental action, but the Supreme Buddha uses it to refer specifically to volitional or intentional action. He says, "It is volition (intentional thought) that I call kamma, for having thought, one acts by body, speech or mind". That being the case, for whatever we think, good or bad, whatever we do and speak, good or bad, kamma is arranged to be experienced and is accumulated all the time.

In His analysis of kamma, the Supreme Buddha points out four types of kamma in the discourse, 'patama kamma sutta'

Bhikkhus, there are four types of kamma that I realized and declared. What four?

01 There are dark kamma with dark results;

02 There are Bright kamma with bright results;

03 There are dark and bright kamma with dark and bright results;

04 There are neither dark nor bright kamma with neither dark nor bright results, which lead to the destruction of kamma.

"Bhikkhus, what are dark actions with dark results?

Here, bhikkhus, a person destroys the life of living beings, takes what is not given, misbehaves in sexual conduct, tells lies and takes intoxicating drinks and drugs.

Bhikkhus, what are bright actions with bright results?

Here, bhikkhus, a person abstains from destroying the life of living beings, taking what is not given, misbehaving in sexual conduct, telling lies and taking intoxicating drinks and drugs.

Bhikkhus, what are dark and bright actions with dark and bright results?

Here, bhikkhus, a person does both good and evil bodily actions, verbal actions and mental actions.

Bhikkhus, what are neither dark nor bright kamma with neither dark nor bright results which lead to the destruction of kamma?

Here, bhikkhus, a person is with right view, right thoughts, right speech, right actions, right livelihood, right effort, right mindfulness and right concentration".

The Supreme Buddha points out three causes for the origination of bad kamma. Greed is a cause for the origination of bad kamma. The word 'greed' is described in many words in Buddhism, such as desire, craving, miserliness, lust, longing and so on. When one thinks, speaks and does something being overcome by greed, the result of that mental, verbal or bodily action will be a bad kamma leading to suffering. Secondly, hatred is a cause for the origination of bad kamma. Anger, animosity, aversion, dislike, ill will, hostility, contempt and so on are synonyms or subordinates that are seen in Buddhist sermons. Overcome by hatred, one may think, speak and act wrongly and he will accumulate bad kamma that will result in suffering.

Thirdly, delusion is a cause for the origination of bad kamma. Because of delusion, one is unable to differentiate between good and bad and he is likely to misunderstand good to be bad and bad to be good. As a result, he gives up what is good and does what is bad. It is just because of delusion that people are of conceit, pride, arrogance and wrong views in this life and life after. Overcome by delusion, one acts wrongly in body, speech and mind generating bad kamma to be experienced. The Supreme Buddha describes greed, hatred and delusion as unwholesome roots from which all the unwholesome kamma arises and potential rebirth in bad worlds could occur.

On the other hand, there are three causes for the origination of good kamma. They are non-greed, non-hatred and non-delusion which may be expressed more positively as generosity, loving kindness and wisdom. Actions springing from these wholesome roots, non-greed, non-hatred and non-delusion, are wholesome kamma leading to happiness to be experienced in the human world or heavenly worlds.

Therefore, beings are responsible for their own misery as well as happiness. No other invisible power creates happiness and misery of beings, but they themselves are the creators of themselves. That is why the Supreme Buddha preached that beings are the owners of their kamma, the heirs to their kamma; they have kamma as their origin, kamma as their relative, kamma as their refuge; whatever kamma they do, good or bad, they are its owners.

(Culakammavibhanga Sutta - MN 3)

The consequences of good or evil kamma are inevitable. The result of the kamma we create ripens in three ways, namely; the results of kamma to be experienced in this very life, or in the next rebirth or on a subsequent occasion. When the suitable conditions come together, the kamma ripens and produces the appropriate results. So, beings have no escape from kamma unless they follow the Dhamma Path. "Man reaps what he had sown, both in the past and in the present. What he sows now, he reaps in the present and in the future".

Being unaware of the fact that one is suffering due to one's own action, people blindly chant and pray for a solution to get rid of their suffering rather than removing the cause of suffering and stop the origination of bad kamma by body, speech and mind to be experienced in future. "If you fear suffering and detest suffering, do not commit any evil deed both openly and secretly".

(Kumaraka Sutta - KN 1)

Kamma plays a decisive role in producing rebirth of beings in due places and the effect it has on beings is undeniable and sometimes very powerful. The Supreme

Buddha, therefore, said in a stanza that : **"The world exists on kamma"**; that is; there is a place called a world as there should be a place for the results of kamma to be given effect.

"The community of beings exists on kamma" That is; human beings, heavenly beings, hell beings, animals and all other beings are born due to kamma. **" Living beings are bound by kamma like the chariot wheel by the pin"**; that is to say that beings never get rid of the endless round of births and deaths as long as this bond between kamma and living beings is not eliminated.

(Vasettha Sutta - MN 2)

The Supreme Buddha pointed to the Noble Eightfold Path, the middle way as the way to eliminate all the kamma and to get free from the samsara, the round of repeated birth and death that has been tied by kamma itself.

Chapter Thirteen

According to the seed that's sown
So is the fruit you reap there from.
Doer of good will gather good
Doer of evil, reaps evil.

- *Isayo Samuddaka Sutta* -

The Fortune and Misfortune of Beings

There is considerable inequality among the human beings living in this world. People are divided as fortunate and unfortunate or superior and inferior on the basis of this inequality. Human beings are seen to be short-lived and long-lived, sickly and healthy, ugly and beautiful, uninfluential and influential, poor and wealthy, low-born and high-born, stupid and wise. Ordinary people, unaware of the fact that the fortune and misfortune of human beings depends on their own kamma, they tend to believe that it happens according to the will or decision of a god or an other external force.

It was the Supreme Buddha who revealed 2600 years ago that one's own kamma is responsible for one's fortune and misfortune. A young man called Suba asked the Blessed One why human beings are seen to be short-lived and long-lived, sickly and healthy, ugly and beautiful, uninfluential and influential, poor and wealthy, low-born and high-born, stupid and wise. The Blessed One explained very clearly how kamma accounts for this inequality. The explanation is as follows.

"Here student, some man or woman kills living beings and is murderous, bloody-handed, merciless to living beings, he or she is engaged in destructing living beings. As a result of their kamma (killing living beings) he takes rebirth in a lower world like hell after death. If he does not reappear in a lower world like hell after death and comes back to the human state, then wherever he is reborn he is short-lived."

"Here student, some man or woman, abandoning the killing of living beings, abstains from killing living beings. He is compassionate to all living beings. As a result of this good conduct and good kamma, he takes rebirth in a happy destination, in a heavenly world, after death. But if he does not reappear in a happy destination after death, he comes back to the human state instead, then wherever he is reborn, he is long-lived."

"Here student, some man or woman harms and injures living beings with a clod, with a stick, with a knife or with the hand. As a result of this (bad) kamma, after death, he reappears in a bad destination like hell. But if he does not reappear in a bad destination like hell and he comes back to the human state instead, wherever he is reborn, he is sickly."

"Here student, some man or woman does not harm and injure living beings with the hand, with a clod, with a stick or with a knife. As a result of this (good) kamma, he takes rebirth in a happy destination like heavenly worlds, after death. But if he does not reappear in a happy destination and he comes back to the human state instead, then wherever he is reborn, he is healthy."

"Here student, some man or woman hates others, gets angry and irritated even when criticised a little, he gets very angry, hostile and resentful and displays anger and hate. As a result of this kamma, after death, he takes rebirth in a bad destination, even in hell. But if he does not take rebirth in a bad destination, after death and he comes back to the human state instead, then wherever he is reborn, he is ugly."

"Here student, some man or woman does not hate others, does not get angry and irritated even when criticised a lot, he does not get angry, hostile and resentful and does not display anger and hate. As a result of this (good) kamma, after death, he reappears in a happy destination, in a heavenly world. But if he does not reappear in a happy destination, he comes back to the human state instead, then wherever he is reborn, he is beautiful."

"Here student, some man or woman is jealous, he envies, resents the gains, honour, respect, reverence, salutations and venerations received by others. As a result of this kamma, after death, he reappears in a bad destination like hell. But if he does not reappear in a bad destination like hell, he comes back to the human state instead, then wherever he is reborn, he is uninfluential."

"Here student, some man or woman is not jealous, he does not envy and resent the gains, honour, respect, reverence, salutations and venerations received by others. As a result of this (good) kamma, after death, he takes rebirth in a happy destination, in a heavenly world. But if he does not reappear in a happy destination after death, he comes back to the human state instead, then wherever he is reborn, he is influential."

"Here student, some man or woman, does not give food, drink, clothing, vehicles, garlands, scents, perfumes, beds, dwelling and lamps to recluses and brahmins.* Because of this kamma, after death, he reappears in a bad destination

*Brahmins are those who are virtuous and of good conduct of the right view and have a concentrated mind and try to be liberated from bonds. Especially the terms, recluses and brahmins, were used by the Supreme Buddha to designate his noble Sangha.

like hell. But if he does not reappear in a bad destination after death, he comes back to the human state instead, then wherever he is reborn, he is poor."

"Here student, some man or woman, gives food, drink, clothing, vehicles, garlands, scents, perfumes, beds, dwelling and lamps to recluses and brahmins. As a result of this good kamma, after death, he takes rebirth in a happy destination, in a heavenly world. But if he does not take rebirth in a happy destination after death, he comes back to the human state instead, then wherever he is reborn, he is wealthy."

"Here student, some man or woman is obstinate and arrogant; he does not pay homage to one who should receive homage, does not rise up for one in whose presence he should rise up, does not offer a seat to one who deserves a seat, does not make way for one for whom he should make way, and does not honour, respect, revere and venerate one who should be honoured, respected, revered and venerated. As a result of such kamma, after death, he reappears in a bad destination, like hell. But if he does not reappear in a bad destination like hell, he comes back to the human state instead, then wherever he is reborn, he is born in low-caste families."

"Here student, some man or woman is not obstinate and arrogant; he pays homage to one who should receive homage, rises up for one in whose presence he should rise up, offer a seat to one who deserves a seat, make way for one whom he should make way, honour, respect, revere and venerate one who should be honoured, respected, revered and venerated. As a result of such (good) kamma, after death, he takes rebirth in a happy destination in the heavenly world. But if he does not take rebirth in a happy destination, he comes back to the human state instead, then wherever he is reborn, he is born in high-caste families."

"Here student, some man or woman does not visit a recluse or a brahmin and asks: Venerable Sir, what is wholesome? What is unwholesome? What is right? What is wrong? What should be cultivated? What should not be cultivated? What kind of action will lead to my harm and suffering for a long time? What kind of action will lead to my welfare and happiness for a long time? As a result of such action, after death he reappears in a bad destination like hell. But if he does not reappear in a bad destination, after death, he comes back to the human state instead, then wherever he is reborn, he is stupid."

"Here student, some man or woman visits a recluse or a Brahmin and ask: Venerable Sir, what is wholesome? What is unwholesome? What is right? What is wrong? What should be cultivated? What should not be cultivated? What kind of action will lead to my harm and suffering for a long time? What kind of action will lead to my welfare and happiness for a long time? As a result of such action, after death, he reappears in a happy destination, in the heavenly world. But if he does not reappear in a happy destination after death, he comes back to the human state instead, then wherever he is reborn, he is wise."

(Culakammavibhanga Sutta - MN 3)

It is now obvious that beings themselves are responsible for their fortune and misfortune. Inequality exists among human beings in this world just because of the particular kamma previously committed by them. No one else or nothing else is responsible for the fortune and misfortune. Therefore, everyone who is exposed to the teachings of the Supreme Buddha should be determined to perform good kamma while following the Noble Eightfold Path leading to the extinction of all kamma.

Chapter Fourteen

Some are born in the womb; evil doers are born in hell;
doers of merits are born in heaven. Noble ones who
abandoned defilements by following the Noble Eightfold
Path attain Nibbāna.

- Dhammapada -

Spontaneous Rebirth

Human beings take rebirth in a mother's womb and the mother gives birth to the baby after nine or ten months. Similarly, animals too are born in an animal mother's womb and are delivered by her after some time. We human beings can witness both these births with our own naked eyes. Apart from these two types of births, there are spontaneous rebirths that we cannot see with our naked eyes. How spontaneous rebirths take place could be seen only by those who have developed a divine eye. The divine eye is gained by way of deeper levels of concentration in their minds, acquired through meditation. The Supreme Buddha, having seen with His divine eye, disclosed those rebirths that take place spontaneously. Beings who are born spontaneously are gods, brahmas, ghosts, hell beings and very rarely human beings like Ambapali, the courtesan.

Gods

Gods are celestial beings. In Pali, they are called devās. They enjoy greater life span, beauty, happiness, glory and power than human beings. They are not immortal beings exercising a creative role in the cosmic process. They have not got rid of the long journey of Samsara, but are subject to suffering, suffering of birth, illness, old age, death and so on. However they are temporarily safe from the lower worlds like hell for a certain period of time. But gods are likely to reappear in a lower world like human beings except for the devas who have won the attainment of 'Sotapanna' (the fruit of stream-entry) and sakadāgāmi (the fruit of once-returning) in a Buddha's dispensation. They have reappeared as gods in the six heavenly worlds as the fruit of the meritorious deeds previously accumulated in the human world. So, their position in the heavenly worlds is not permanent. As they are not freed from bondage and craving like human beings, they equally stand in need of guidance from the Supreme Buddha who is the teacher of both gods and humans (Satta deva manussānam).

Unlike human beings, devas have a high level of intelligence. This means if they get the chance to listen to the Buddha Dhamma, they are capable of realising it very soon. Specifically, the gods who have practised the Dhamma very well while they were in the human world understand it more quickly than other gods. In the six heavenly worlds, there are hundreds of millions of gods who have attained the stages of stream-entry and once returning under the guidance of the Supreme Buddha, Gautama. They are practising the Dhamma further to attain the final goal, Arahantship- the complete freedom from all suffering. The path leading to the heavens is the Three Refuges - the Buddha, Dhamma and Sangha or the confidence in them and various meritorious deeds done based on the worldly Right View.

It is said that the human beings who honestly live by the Dhamma are protected by the devās and receive their blessings. It is a Buddhist custom to share the merits of good deeds with gods, such as giving alms to the noble Sangha, Dhamma preaching and listening, making offerings to the Supreme Buddha and many other meritorious deeds. Buddhists never worship and pray to devās wishing for happiness, prosperity, good health, an end of suffering and so on. Instead, they only share the merits of good deeds with them and expect their protection.

Human beings who honestly live by the Dhamma but fail to realise it, no matter how much they strive, get another opportunity to realise it in a heavenly world. Therefore, the Supreme Buddha stressed the importance of accumulating more and more merits by mind, body and speech and living by the Dhamma. One, for this purpose, should firmly establish himself on the Three Refuges, the Buddha, Dhamma and Sangha.

Brahmas

Above the six deva worlds, there is another realm called 'the form realm'. The inhabitants of these worlds are also devās. In order to distinguish from the devās in the six heavenly worlds, they are known as brahmas and the place they dwell is called the brahma world. Brahmas have a subtler form than that of the devās. Beings are reborn in brahma worlds spontaneously as a result of the four jhanas or meditative absorptions developed in the human or deva worlds. Accordingly, the brahmas experience meditative bliss rather than sensual pleasure because the meditator abandons the sensual desire when he reaches Jhanas.

At the very top of these brahma worlds are the five 'Pure Abodes' (Suddhāvāsa), the places of rebirth accessible only to non-returners. The life span of the Brahmas is far longer than that of devās. Except for non-returners who attain Nibbāna fully in the five 'Pure abodes' themselves, other brahmas are wanderers in the journey of Samsara. They are likely to be reborn even in the lower worlds at the end of their life span. It means that their roles as brahmas are not eternal or permanent. However, as they are endowed with must merit power, they are too capable of realising the Dhamma very quickly the devās. The Supreme Buddha is the teacher of both devās and brahmas. Millions of brahmas who listened to the Blessed One's Dhamma got liberated from samsaric journey for good.

Ghosts

The above mentioned spontaneous rebirths in the deva worlds and brahma worlds belong to the heavenly worlds where there is extreme happiness. Apart from them, another spontaneous rebirth is the rebirth as ghosts. Westerners have a different perspective on ghosts. The notions of ghosts they have made according to what they have heard, seen and felt are true to some extent. It was the Supreme Buddha who provided the detailed facts about the ghosts after having understood this world and the next with his direct knowledge.

The Pali term for ghost is 'petha' and the English terms for ghost meaning spirit, apparition, spectre or spook does not imply the exact meaning of the Pali term 'petha'. However, pethas are also helpless beings who are wandering on and entangled in the samsaric journey full of suffering. Most of them with a few exceptions have six sense bases: eyes, ears, nose, a tongue, a body and mind. They have no intelligence and no capacity to think wisely and act accordingly. They are afflicted beings in utter misery. They have to undergo extreme suffering due to their own sinful deeds, immoral conduct, intense desire for sensual pleasures, ferocious anger, excessive greed and so on.

Beings in the ghost world do not farm, herd cattle, trade, buy, sell or use gold and money. Some ghosts survive from merits shared by humans. Most of them suffer from overwhelming hunger and thirst and are tired and wailing miserably and desperately. Due to the bad kamma of ghosts, the only foods they deserve are phlegm, saliva, mucus, pus, excrement and urine passed from human bodies. Some are overcome by hunger and thirst and travel many miles searching for food and water but they cannot find any. They faint and fall on the ground on their backs and face down. Some ghosts who have been born in cesspits eat the filth full of worms.

Ghosts can not be seen with our naked eyes as they do not have a gross form like ours. Only the Buddha and some Arahants who gained the divine eye could see them. Most ghosts are naked. Ghosts have an awful, nasty appearance and are very ugly, their veins are popping out, and their ribs are sticking out. According to the size and the gravity of the kamma accumulated, the ghosts experience suffering in different ways. Some are pierced by needles, spread burning hay and embers on their head by themselves, hit themselves on the head with an iron rod, eat their own flesh and blood and dogs tear off their flesh. Also, there are ghosts who fight each other using hammers and drink the blood and pus of their victims.

The Supreme Buddha revealed that after human beings, due to their bad kamma are born in the ghost world, they will come back to their own houses and stand by the doors, outside the walls and at intersections. Unlike humans, ghosts can see what they did to suffer in the ghost world. They also see the hells if they are to be reborn in next life in order to aggravate their suffering. The life span of ghosts is very long and they have to suffer intensely in this way for many hundred years, millions years and sometime for aeons. Most of the ghosts are reborn in the same ghost world again while many other ghosts are reborn in hell and the animal world.

Hell Beings

Beings who have committed grave sinful deeds are born in hell (niraya in Pali) spontaneously. Out of bad destinations, hell is the place where beings receive the most rigorous punishment for their sinful deeds. There are numerous hells and the punishment hell beings receive is different in each hell. Most of the time, hell beings have to experience punishment in a number of hells once they appear in hell due to grave sinful deeds committed by them. Some of the sinful deeds, for example, are ill-treating and killing parents, sexual misconduct, insulting and harassing the Buddha, Arahants and virtuous persons and so on. Hell is so dangerous that hell beings have to suffer there for aeons and aeons with no end in sight.

The Supreme Buddha said that the suffering in hell is so much so that it is hard to find a simile to describe it. When a bhikkhu asked Him to give a simile, He said thus: "Bhikkhus, suppose men caught a robber culprit and presented him to the king, saying: 'Sire, here is a robber culprit. Order what punishment you will for him. Then the king said: 'Go and strike this man in the morning with a hundred spears.' And they struck him in the morning with a hundred spears. Then at noon the king asked: 'How is that man?' 'Sire, he is still alive.' Then the king said: 'Go and strike that man at noon with a hundred spears.' And they struck him at noon with a hundred spears. Then in the evening the king asked: 'How is that man?' 'Sire, he is still alive.' Then the king said: 'Go and strike that man in the evening with a hundred spears.' And they struck him in the evening with a hundred spears.

What do you think, bhikkhus? Would that man experience pain and grief because of being struck with the three hundred spears?" "Venerable sir, that man would experience pain and grief because of being struck with even one spear, let alone three hundred."

Then, taking a small stone the size of his hand, the Blessed One addressed the bhikkhus thus: "What do you think, bhikkhus? Which is the greater, this small stone that I have taken, the size of my hand, or Himalaya, the king of mountains?" "Venerable sir, the small stone that the Blessed One has taken, the size of his hand, does not count beside Himalaya, the king of mountains; it is not even a fraction, there is no comparison." "So too, bhikkhus, the pain and grief that the man would experience because of being struck with the three hundred spears does not count beside the suffering of hell; it is not even a fraction, there is no comparison."

(Balapandita Sutta - MN 3)

Note: - For more details about the hell please read the Devaduta Sutta (The Divine Messengers) in the Middle Length Discourses of the Buddha.

The Supreme Buddha, the only one who saw the hell world with his divine eye, mentioned that beings who hold 'wrong view' are destined to be reborn in hell as well.

Out of all the hells, the hell called 'Avīchi' is the most dangerous hell. It is said that Avīchi is the most densely populated out of all the realms (that is, heavenly worlds, brahma worlds, animal world, human world and other hells)

The tragic and pathetic life the ghosts and hell beings experience is due to their own bad kamma. Every action has its result. None can escape from kamma committed by themselves. Therefore, it is advisable to restrain the three doors-mind, body and speech- and practise generosity. Also, one should be virtuous by keeping five precepts. Furthermore, one should try to develop the mind by means of meditation. Briefly, one should live by the teachings of the Supreme Buddha in order to escape from a bad world like this.

Chapter Fifteen

Of those things that arise from a cause
The Tathagata the Buddha has told the cause,
And also what their cessation is
This is the doctrine of the Great (the Buddha)

- *The Arahant Venerable Assajī* -

Dependent Origination

Dependent origination (Paticca-Samuppāda) is one of the central teachings of the Buddha. The Supreme Buddha who realised this profound Dhamma expounded it in a sequence of twelve factors. This unique discovery reveals how suffering is originated in a casual pattern and how suffering entirely comes to a halt by going against that very pattern. The arising of dependent origination is the continuation of what we call 'Samsara', the round of rebirths and the cessation of dependent origination is the end of that endless round.

Understanding of the arising and cessation of dependent origination enables one to keep clear of the two extreme views, namely: eternalism and annihilationism. Eternalism holds that there is a permanent self which transmigrates from one life to the next while retaining a personal identity. When the cessation of dependent origination is understood, this extreme is removed. Annihilationism holds that there is no life after death, and the present life at death is entirely destroyed and annihilated. This extreme is cut off when the arising of dependent origination is understood. This Dhamma, dependent origination gives a very clear-cut understanding about the whole teaching of the Supreme Buddha. It is manifest in his saying, "One who sees the dependent origination sees the Dhamma, and one who sees the Dhamma sees the dependent origination".

The ultimate purpose of the teaching on dependent origination is to explain very clearly the conditions that give rise to suffering so as to show what must be done to gain release from all suffering. Dependent origination, the greatest discovery ever in human history, unravels the mysterious mechanism that perpetuates suffering indefinitely into the future with no end in sight. By breaking up this mechanism at the time of the Enlightenment, the Supreme Buddha got rid of suffering forever, and expounded that suffering is due to a cause. This mutual interdependence forms the theory of dependent origination thus; "when this exists, that comes to be; with the arising of this, that arises. When this does not exist, that does not come to be; with the cessation of this, that ceases."

(Cula sakuludai Sutta - MN 2)

Arising of Dependent Origination (Causality)

Dependent on ignorance, arises formations.

Dependent on formations, arises consciousness.

Dependent of consciousness, arises mentality-materiality.

Dependent on mentality-materiality, arises the six-sense bases.

Dependent on six-sense bases, arises contact.

Dependent on contact, arises feeling.

Dependent on feeling, arises craving

Dependent on craving, arises clinging

Dependent on clinging, arises the arranging of kamma.

Dependent on the arranging of kamma, arises birth

Dependent on the birth, arises ageing, death, sorrows, lamentation, pain, grief and despair.

Thus, there is the arising of this whole mass of suffering.

Cessation of Dependent Origination.

Through the entire cessation of ignorance, formation ceases,

Through the cessation of formation, consciousness ceases,

Through the cessation of consciousness, mentality and materiality cease,

Through the cessation of mentality and materiality, the six sense bases cease,

Through the cessation of the six sense bases, contact ceases,

Through the cessation of contact, feeling ceases,

Through the cessation of feeling, craving ceases,

Through the cessation of craving, clinging ceases,

Through the cessation of clinging, the arranging of kamma ceases,

Through the cessation of the arranging of kamma, birth ceases

Through the cessation of birth, ageing, death, sorrow, lamentation, pain, grief and despair ceases,

Thus, there is the cessation of this whole mass of suffering.

Explanation of the Factors of Dependant Origination.

1. Ignorance (Avijja) – Not knowing suffering, not knowing the origin of suffering, not knowing the cessation of suffering, not knowing the way leading to the cessation of suffering,

2. Formation (*Sankara*)- There are three formations. The bodily formation; that is in-breathing and out-breathing. As breathing in and out is connected with body, they are called bodily formations.

The verbal formation; that is thinking (Vitakka) and re-thinking (Vicara) Before uttering a word first, one thinks and re-thinks and subsequently speaks. Therefore, Vitakka and Vicara (thinking and re-thinking) are verbal formations.

The mental formation; that is perception (to recognise who, what, etc and feeling. Perception and feeling are mental; these states are states bound up with the mind; therefore, perception (Sañña) and feeling (Vēdanā) are mental formations.

3. Consciousness (Viññana) – that is, to know or to cognise. The eye gets to know forms, the ear gets to know sounds, the nose gets to know smells, the tongue gets to know tastes, the body gets to know touches and the mind gets to know thoughts. There are six classes of consciousness: eye-consciousness, ear-consciousness, nose-consciousness, tongue-consciousness, body consciousness, mind consciousness (Consciousness can also be termed as the stream of consciousness in the sense that it passes on from one life to a new existence.)

4. Mentality–materiality (also name and form) - Feelings (Vēdana), perception (Sañña), volition (Cetana), contact (Phassa) and attention (Manasikāra); this is called 'mentality'. The four great elements (earth, water, heat, air) and the form derived from the four great elements: this is called materiality.

5. The six- sense bases (Salāyatana) - that is: eye, ear, nose, tongue, body and mind.

6. Contact (Phassa) - there are six classes of contact;

eye contact, ear-contact, nose-contact, tongue-contact, body-contact, mind-contact. Eye-contact arises when three things get together: eye, form (a visible object) and consciousness. Ear-contact arises when ear, sound and consciousness come together. Nose–contact arises when nose, smell and consciousness come together. Tongue–contact arises when tongue, taste and consciousness come together. Body – contact arises when body, touch and consciousness come together. Mind – contact arises when the mind, thought and consciousness come together.

7. Feeling (Vedana) – there are six classes of feeling: feeling born of eye contact, feeling born of ear-contact, feeling born of nose contact, feeling born of tongue-contact, feeling born of body-contact, feeling born of mind-contact. There are three kinds of feelings: pleasant feeling, painful feeling and neither-painful-nor-pleasant feeling. When, for example, the eye meets a form, e.g. a man, woman, flower etc., eye–consciousness arises. Because of the meeting of these three, eye-contact arises. Out of the eye-contact a pleasant feeling is born if the form that the eye meets is an agreeable one, a painful feeling is born if the form is a disagreeable one and a neither-painful-nor-pleasant feeling is born if the form is a neither-agreeable-nor-disagreeable one.

8. Craving (Tanha) – There are six classes of craving: Craving for forms, craving for sounds, craving for smells, craving for tastes, craving for touches, craving for thoughts.

9. Clinging (Upādāna) – There are four kinds of clinging: clinging to sensual pleasures, clinging to (wrong)

views (about the world, Nibbāna etc.) clinging to wrong disciplinary rules and observances (followed in the belief that they can bring purification), and clinging to wrong concept of a self.

10. Arranging of kamma (Bhava) – Kamma is arranged in three ways, kamma is arranged for a birth in sense- sphere existence, kamma is arranged for a birth in form-sphere existence and kamma is arranged for a birth in formless-sphere existence.

11. Birth (Jāti) – Birth takes place according to the arranging of kamma in particular existences.

12. Because of birth, ageing,death,sorrow, lamentation,pain,grief and despair arise.

————————————————

Chapter Sixteen

Few among human beings are those who cross samsara
and attain Nibbāna. The rest, the bulk of people return to
Samsara, the near shore.

- *Dhammapada* -

Samsara is dangerous

Samsāra is the continuous process of being born, growing old and dying again and again. Many believe that there is no life after death. But it is a mere belief. Our journey will continue infinitely into the future with no end in sight, as long as ignorance and craving remain intact. Craving and ignorance are the roots in this cycle of births. The great Compassionate One, the Supreme Buddha said that this samsāra in which the beings are entangled, is without discoverable beginning. A starting point cannot be seen of beings roaming and wandering on, covered by ignorance and tied by craving.

What is the problem beings have to face in the long journey of samsāra? Briefly, the answer is suffering. Suffering is because this samsāra is not made up of only this human world and heavenly worlds but also of very dangerous places like hell, the animal world, the ghost world and so on. The beings who are unaware of the danger existing in this samsāra are reborn in these bad worlds again and again. Those lower worlds are the most frequented places of the beings wandering on in this long samsāra.

It is extremely rare that they come to the human world or a heavenly world. Even in the human world, how much suffering humans experience from birth to death? Dangerous and incurable diseases, droughts, natural disasters, shortage of resources, religious and economic issues, wars and so many different problems are some of the matters which cause a lot of suffering.

After having confronted this mass of suffering, humans, after death, take rebirth among the animals, ghosts and even in hell according to their action (kamma). Needless to mention the suffering experienced by the beings in the bad worlds. They are helpless with no one to rescue them. There is no escape in sight for an exceedingly long time. This is the inherent nature of the dangerous, fearful Samsāra whether human beings accept it or not.

The people in this world do not pause for a while to think of this danger because they do not see the danger of Samsāra beyond this human world. More to the point, they do not hear this message which is announced only by the Buddhas, who very rarely appear in this world. Only a very few human beings endowed with previously accumulated, enormous merits hear of Samsāra and its suffering and get liberated from it forever. All other beings blinded by wrong faiths, intoxicated with sensual pleasure, and driven by material wealth and power use up the very rare and valuable human life with no use, as if there were no life hereafter. At the end they end up in a lower world full of suffering as they have no merit left to be born in a good world. At that moment, they see the real nature of samsāra but then it is too late.

Only the Supreme Buddha sees this pathetic side of the samsāra and discloses it with great compassion to heavenly and human beings in order for them to get rid of it forever. This marvellous revelation makes the wise heavenly and human beings who are stuck in the mire of samsāra become disenchanted, disgusted and dispassionate towards this horrifying endless journey full of suffering. Given below are some quotations from the discourses on "Without Discoverable Beginning" referring to the samsāra.

Mothers

"Bhikkhus, this samsāra is without discoverable beginning. A starting point is not discerned of beings roaming and wandering on hindered by ignorance and fettered by craving. Suppose, bhikkhus, a man would cut up whatever grass, sticks, branches, and foliage there are in this Jambudipa (India) and collect them together into a single heap. Having done so, he would put them down, saying (for each one): 'This is my mother, this my mother's mother.' The sequence of that man's mothers and grandmothers would not come to an end, yet the grass, wood, branches, and foliage in this Jambudipa (India) would be used up and exhausted. For what reason? Because, bhikkhus, this samsāra is without discoverable beginning.

The Earth

Suppose, bhikkhus, a man would reduce this great earth to balls of clay to the size of olives and put them down, saying (for each one): 'this is my father, this is my father's father.' The sequence of that man's fathers and grandfathers would not come to an end, yet this great earth would be used up and exhausted. For what reason? Because, bhikkhus, this samsāra is without discoverable beginning.

Tears

What do you think, bhikkhus, which is more: the stream of tears that you have shed as you roamed and wandered on through this long course, weeping and wailing because of being united with the disagreeable and separated from the agreeable - this or the water in the four great oceans?

"As we understand the Dhamma taught by the Blessed One, venerable sir, the stream of tears that we have shed as we roamed and wandered through this long course, weeping and wailing because of being united with the disagreeable and separated from the agreeable-this alone is more than the water in the four great oceans."

"Good, good, bhikkhus! It is good that you understand the Dhamma taught by me in such a way. The stream of tears that you have shed as you roamed and wandered through this long course, weeping and wailing because of being united with the disagreeable and separated from the agreeable this alone is more than the water in the four great oceans. For a long time, bhikkhus, you have experienced the death of a mother. As you have experienced this, weeping and wailing because of being united with the disagreeable and separated from the agreeable, the stream of tears that you have shed is more than the water in the four great oceans.

"For a long time, bhikkhus, you have experienced the death of a father... the death of a brother... the death of a sister... the death of a son... the death of a daughter... the loss of relatives... the loss of wealth… loss through illness. As you have experienced this, weeping and wailing because of being united with the disagreeable and separated from the agreeable, the stream of tears that you have shed is more than the water in the four great oceans. For what reason? Because, bhikkhus, this samsāra is without discoverable beginning.

Mother's Milk

"What do you think, bhikkhus, which is more: the mother's milk that you have drunk as you roamed and wandered through this long course - this or the water in the four great oceans?"

"As we understand the Dhamma taught by the Blessed One, venerable sir, the mother's milk that we have drunk as we roamed and wandered on through this long course - this alone is more than the water in the four great oceans."

"Good, good, bhikkhus! It is good that you understand the Dhamma taught by me in such a way. The mother's milk that you have drunk as you roamed and wandered through this long course - this alone is more than the water in the four great oceans. For what reason? Because, bhikkhus, this saṃsāra is without discoverable beginning..."

Unfortunate

Whenever you see anyone in misfortune, in misery, you can conclude: 'We too have experienced the same thing in this long course.' For what reason? Because, bhikkhus, this saṃsāra is without discoverable beginning...

Happy

Whenever you see anyone happy and fortunate, you can conclude: 'We too have experienced the same thing in this long course.' For what reason? Because, bhikkhus, this saṃsāra is without discoverable beginning....

Thirty Bhikkhus

What do you think, bhikkhus, which is more: the stream of blood that you have shed when you were beheaded as you roamed and wandered on through this long course - this or the water in the four great oceans?"

"As we understand the Dhamma taught by the Blessed One, venerable sir, the stream of blood that we have shed when our heads were cut off as we roamed and wandered on through this long course - this alone is more than the water in the four great oceans."

"Good, good, bhikkhus! It is good that you understand the Dhamma taught by me in such a way. The stream of blood that you have shed as you roamed and wandered on through this long course - this alone is more than the water in the four great oceans. For a long time, bhikkhus, you have been cows, and when as cows you were beheaded, the stream of blood that you shed is greater than the waters in the four great oceans. For a long time you have been buffaloes, sheep, goats, deer, chickens, and pigs.... For a long time you have been arrested as burglars, highwaymen, and adulterers, and when you were beheaded, the stream of blood that you shed is greater than the water in the four great oceans. For what reason? Because, bhikkhus, this samsāra is without discoverable beginning."

(Anamatagga Samyutta - SN 2)

These discourses awaken us to the fact that samsara is not a safe place for us to remain. The journey of samsara is just like a walk in the thick darkness without a torch. Any tragic incident is possible at any time. Likewise, the danger that the beings who wander through this samsara is the four bad destinations. Therefore, it is advisable to immediately follow the teachings of the Supreme Buddha which clearly show the way leading to the end of Samsāra.

Chapter Seventeen

Having obtained the human state
When the good Dhamma has been well proclaimed
Those who do not seize the moment
Have let the right moment slip by.

- *Akkhana Sutta* -

Do Not Miss This Moment

The Supreme Buddha, the great teacher of both gods and humans, preached that it is hard to be born a human being (Kiccho manussapatilābo). Rarely does a being come to the human world after having suffered in bad realms like hell for aeons. And also, out of the human beings who pass away, only a few of them are reborn again in the human world and heavenly worlds. Thus, birth as a human being is a rare thing in the world. Even rarer than the human rebirth is the appearance of a Buddha in the world (Kiccho Buddhānam uppādo). It is because it takes aeons and aeons to fulfil the required merits to become a Buddha. Just because the arising of a Buddha is rare in the world, it is hard to gain the opportunity to hear the sublime Dhamma proclaimed by a Buddha (Kiccham Saddammasavanam).

The rarest thing is the coincidence of the human rebirth and the arising of the Buddhas which is called the 'opportune moment' (*Akkhana*) in the Dhamma. Extremely rarely does a human being who rarely comes to this world encounter a Buddha or gain the opportunity to hear His Dhamma. If one understands the rarity of this moment after having wisely considered the teachings of the Buddha, then he enters the path that leads him to the end of suffering completely. However, there are eight inopportune moments that are not right occasions for following the teachings of the Buddha. They are as follows:

1. A Buddha has appeared in the world and the Dhamma leading to enlightenment and freedom from suffering is taught

as proclaimed by the Buddha. But a person has been reborn in hell. The person born in hell does not get the chance to listen to the Dhamma. Hell is a place where beings are savagely punished constantly for the grave bad kamma committed when in the human world. This is the first inopportune moment for following the teachings of the Buddha.

2. A Buddha has appeared in the world and the Dhamma leading to enlightenment and freedom from suffering is taught as proclaimed by the Buddha. But a person has been reborn in the animal realm due to bad Kamma. Animals though they happen to hear the Dhamma do not understand the Dhamma as they have no intelligence at all. This is the second inopportune moment for following the teaching of the Buddha.

3. A Buddha has appeared in the world and the Dhamma leading to enlightenment and freedom from suffering is taught as proclaimed by the Buddha. But a person has been reborn in the ghost world owing to bad Kamma. There, ghosts are incessantly suffering from thirst, hunger, and other rigorous punishments and they have confused minds. Therefore, they do not have capacity to understand the sublime Dhamma. This is the third inopportune moment that is not right occasion for following the teachings of the Buddha.

4. A Buddha has appeared in the world and the Dhamma leading to enlightenment and freedom from suffering is taught as proclaimed by the Buddha. But a person has been reborn in a certain order of long - lived devas (in the order of non-percipient devas who cannot see, hear, notice and feel anything). Those devas, therefore, miss the

rare chance of getting liberated from suffering. This is the forth inopportune moment that is not the right occasion for following the teachings of the Buddha.

5. A Buddha has appeared in the world and the Dhamma leading to enlightenment and freedom from suffering is taught as proclaimed by the Buddha. But a person has been reborn in the outlying countries (beyond the Indian subcontinent) where bhikkus, bhikkhunis, male lay followers, and female lay followers do not travel. Therefore, that person born in far off countries do not hear the Dhamma. This is the fifth inopportune moment that is not the right occasion for following the teachings of the Buddha.

6. A Buddha has appeared in the world and the Dhamma leading to enlightenment and freedom from suffering is taught as proclaimed by the Buddha. A person has been reborn in the central part of the India where the Buddhas appear, but he holds wrong view: there are no results in giving, there are no results in helping and giving service to others, there are no results in veneration and making offerings, there are no fruit and result in good and bad kamma, there is no place called 'this world', there is no place called other world, there is no special person called mother, there is no special person called father, there are no beings who are born spontaneously, there are no good and virtuous recluses and brahmins in the world who have conquered this world and the other world by themselves through their own knowledge. Such a person is never prepared to listen to the Dhamma and therefore misses the great opportunity. This is the sixth inopportune moment that is not the right occasion for following the path of the Dhamma.

7. A Buddha has appeared in the world and the Dhamma leading to enlightenment and freedom from suffering is taught as proclaimed by the Buddha. A person has been reborn in the central part of India where the Buddhas appear, but he is unwise and unable to understand the meaning of the Dhamma. This is the seventh inopportune moment that is not the right occasion for following the path of the Dhamma.

8. A Buddha has not arisen in the world and the Dhamma leading to enlightenment and freedom from suffering is not taught as proclaimed by the Buddha. But a person has been reborn in the central part of India, and he is wise, intelligent and able to understand the meaning of the Dhamma. Though he is a wise person, a Buddha has not arisen to teach the Dhamma. This is the eighth inopportune moment that is not the right occasion for following the path of the Dhamma.

(Akkhana Sutta - AN 5)

The Supreme Buddha mentioned that there is only one opportunity and only one unique opportune moment for following the path of the Dhamma leading to Nibbāna. That is; a Buddha has arisen in the world and the Dhamma leading to enlightenment and freedom from suffering is taught as proclaimed by the Buddha, and a person has been reborn in the central part of India where Buddhas arise and His Dhamma is taught. That person is wise, intelligent and able to understand the meanings of the Dhamma. This is the only one unique opportune moment to follow the path of the Dhamma and realise its ultimate goal of Nibbāna.

Anyone who has gained the opportunity to hear and read this Dhamma leading to freedom from suffering is of course a fortunate one. He has the rare chance of building confidence in this Dhamma, thereby following the path to the end of suffering. Therefore, regardless of what you are and what you believe it is good to take the initiative as soon as possible before the moment slips by. Those who miss this moment grieve when they are reborn in hell and regret for a long time like a merchant who has missed a profit. The Supreme Buddha also said that those who have failed in the good Dhamma will long experience endless suffering in the round of birth and death.

May all who hear and read this message of the Buddha strive hard and make the best use of the moment and get liberated from all the suffering forever!

Chapter Eighteen

The monk who radiates loving kindness and is deeply
devoted to the teachings of the Buddhas attains the peace of
Nibbāna, the bliss of the cessation of conditioned things.

- Dhammapada -

Loving Kindness Meditation

Loving kindness (Metta in Pali) means the friendliness that is extended wholeheartedly towards oneself as well as others. If one is a true friend to oneself, he does not do any harm to himself and if one is a true friend to others, he does not do any harm to them as well. Therefore, the friendliness that does good to both oneself and others alike is called loving kindness.

As a subject of meditation, loving kindness is of course a great source of generating merits. If someone were to give away a hundred large pots of boiled rice as charity in the morning, a hundred large pots of boiled rice as charity at noon, and a hundred large pots of boiled rice as charity in the evening, and if someone else were to develop a mind of loving kindness even for the time it takes to pull a cow's udder, either in the morning, at noon or in the evening, this would be more fruitful than the former. *(Okkhasata Sutta - SN 1)* Hence, the Supreme Buddha encouraged the disciples to radiate loving kindness whenever possible. The one who develops a mind of loving kindness is enormously protected from non-human beings. It is mentioned in the Dhamma that one who practises loving kindness meditation is just like a sword, and therefore if he is going to be attacked by a non-human, that being itself would have to experience adverse effects.

The Supreme Buddha prescribed the loving kindness meditation as a way of abandoning anger. If a person overcome by anger suffers a lot, the only and infallible remedy is to practise loving kindness meditation. If one develops loving kindness meditation very well, he will be able to completely eradicate anger in a way that it never arises again. In the Sutta named 'Karajakaya', the Supreme Buddha vividly explains how one's old bad kamma committed in this life is worn away by loving kindness meditation. Loving kindness is such a powerful subject of meditation that the meditator can become a non-returner (anāgāmi) who will spontaneously be reborn in a special realm called 'Pure Abodes' and attain the final fruit of Nibbāna, the Arahantship without returning from that world.

The Supreme Buddha has taught eleven benefits of loving kindness. They are as follows:

1. One sleeps well.

2. One wakes up happily.

3. One does not see bad dreams.

4. One is pleasant to human beings.

5. One is pleasant to non-human beings.

6. Deities protect him.

7. Fire, poison and weapons do not harm him.

8. One's mind quickly becomes concentrated.

9. One's facial complexion becomes serene.

10. One dies unconfused.

11. If one is unable to attain Arahantship in this life, he will be born in the brahma world after death.

(Mettanisansa Sutta - AN 6)

And also, The Supreme Buddha has described the power of result produced by developing loving kindness meditation in the sutta "Do not fear merits"

"Bhikkhus, do not fear meritorious deeds. This is an expression denoting happiness, what is desirable, wished for, dear and agreeable, that is, 'meritorious deeds.' For I know full well, bhikkhus, that for a long time I experienced desirable, wished for, dear and agreeable results from often performing meritorious deeds.

"Having cultivated for seven years a mind of loving-kindness, for seven aeons of contraction and expansion I did not return to this world. Whenever the aeon contracted, I reached the plane of Streaming Radiance (Abhassara brahma world), and when the aeon expanded, I arose in an empty Brahma-mansion. And there I was a Brahmā, the Great Brahmā, the Unvanquished Victor, the All-seeing, the All-powerful, the one who realized everything and I took everything under my control. Thirty-six times I was Sakka, the ruler of the devas. And many hundreds of times I was a Wheel-turning Monarch, righteous, a king of righteousness, conqueror of the four quarters of the earth, maintaining stability in the land, in possession of the seven jewels. It is needless to mention of mere local kingship.

"It occurred to me, bhikkhus, to wonder: 'Of what kind of deed of mine is this the fruit? Of what deed's ripening is it that I am now of such great accomplishment and power?' And then it occurred to me: 'It is the fruit of three kinds of deeds of mine, the ripening of three kinds of deeds that I am now of such great accomplishment and power: Then I realized this: they are deeds of giving, of self-restraint, and disciplining mind, body and speech"

One should train in deeds of merit
That yield long-lasting happiness:
Generosity, a peaceful balanced life,
Developing a loving mind.

By cultivating these three things,
Deeds yielding happiness,
The wise person is reborn in heaven
In an untroubled happy world.

(*Ma Punnabhai Sutta - KN 1*)

According to the Dhamma, there are two ways of practising loving kindness.

1. The Exalted Deliverance of Mind (*Mahaggata Chēto Vimukti*)

Here, the meditator starts radiating loving-kindness first to himself and next to all beings where he is (be it at home, in the office, etc) and then to all beings in the village, town, county, country, world and the universe respectively. In this way the meditator spreads loving-kindness by gradually enlarging the size of the area. The more the size of the area one radiates loving kindness to, the more the merits he gathers. If he wishes, he could spread loving-kindness continuously only to a certain area he selects (for example, "to all beings in this village")

2. The immeasurable Deliverance of Mind (*Appamāna Chēto Vimukti*)

Here, loving-kindness is spread direction wise. The meditator starts radiating loving-kindness first to himself and then, he spreads loving kindness to the main compass points and those in between.

Mettha Bhāvanā - Loving Kindness Meditation

May I be free from anger.
May I be free from ill will.
May I be free from jealousy.
May I be free from mental suffering.
May I be free from physical suffering.
May I live in peace.
May I live happily.

May I be free from anger.
May I be free from ill will.
May I be free from jealousy.
May I be free from mental suffering.
May I be free from physical suffering.
May I live in peace.
May I live happily.

May my parents, teachers, relatives and my friends; may all
beings in this house:
... be free from anger.
... be free from ill will.
... be free from jealousy.
... be free from mental suffering.
... be free from physical suffering.
May all beings in this house live in peace.
May all being in this house live happily.

May all beings in this village:
... be free from anger.
... be free from ill will.

... be free from jealousy.

... be free from mental suffering.

... be free from physical suffering.

May all beings in this village live in peace.

May all beings in this village live happily.

May all beings in this city:

... be free from anger.

... be free from ill will.

... be free from jealousy.

... be free from mental suffering.

... be free from physical suffering.

May all beings in this city live in peace.

May all beings in this city live happily.

May all beings in this province:

... be free from anger

... be free from ill will.

... be free from jealousy.

... be free from mental suffering.

... be free from physical suffering.

May all beings in this province live in peace.

May all beings in this province live happily.

May all beings in this country:

... be free from anger.

... be free from ill will.

... be free from jealousy.

... be free from mental suffering

. .. be free from physical suffering.

May all beings in this country live in peace.

May all beings in this country live happily.

May all beings in this world:
... be free from anger.
... be free from ill will.
... be free from jealousy.
... be free from mental suffering.
... be free from physical suffering.
May all beings in this world live in peace.
May all beings in this world live happily... live happily... live happily

May all beings:
...be free from anger.
... be free from ill will.
... be free from jealousy.
... be free from mental suffering.
... be free from physical suffering.
May all beings live in peace.
May all beings live happily... live happily... live happily

May all beings in the North direction;
...be free from anger.
... be free from ill will.
... be free from jealousy.
... be free from mental suffering.
... be free from physical suffering.
May all beings live in peace.
May all beings live happily... live happily... live happily

May all beings in the Northeast direction;

...be free from anger.

... be free from ill will.

... be free from jealousy.

... be free from mental suffering.

... be free from physical suffering.

May all beings live in peace.

May all beings live happily... live happily... live happily

May all beings in the East direction;

...be free from anger.

... be free from ill will.

... be free from jealousy.

... be free from mental suffering.

... be free from physical suffering.

May all beings live in peace.

May all beings live happily... live happily... live happily

May all beings in the Southeast direction;

...be free from anger.

... be free from ill will.

... be free from jealousy.

... be free from mental suffering.

... be free from physical suffering.

May all beings live in peace.

May all beings live happily... live happily... live happily

May all beings in the South direction;

...be free from anger.

... be free from ill will.

... be free from jealousy.

... be free from mental suffering.

... be free from physical suffering.
May all beings live in peace.
May all beings live happily... live happily... live happily

May all beings in the Southwest direction;
...be free from anger.
... be free from ill will.
... be free from jealousy.
... be free from mental suffering.
... be free from physical suffering.
May all beings live in peace.
May all beings live happily... live happily... live happily

May all beings in the West direction;
...be free from anger.
... be free from ill will.
... be free from jealousy.
... be free from mental suffering.
... be free from physical suffering.
May all beings live in peace.
May all beings live happily... live happily... live happily

May all beings in the Northwest direction;
...be free from anger.
... be free from ill will.
... be free from jealousy.
... be free from mental suffering.
... be free from physical suffering.
May all beings live in peace.
May all beings live happily... live happily... live happily

May all beings in the above;
…be free from anger.
... be free from ill will.
... be free from jealousy.
... be free from mental suffering.
... be free from physical suffering.
May all beings live in peace.
May all beings live happily... live happily... live happily

May all beings in the below;
…be free from anger.
... be free from ill will.
... be free from jealousy.
... be free from mental suffering.
... be free from physical suffering.
May all beings live in peace.
May all beings live happily... live happily... live happily

Sādhu! Sādhu! Sādhu!

Chapter Nineteen

To support one's father and mother, to cherish one's wife and children and to be engaged in peaceful occupations, these are the highest blessings.

- *Mahā Mangala Sutta* -

The Value of Parents

Parents are those who gave us life and nurtured us. Also, it is our parents who raised us up until we are capable of doing our jobs and taking responsibilities. In the struggle of bringing up their children, they have gone through hard times even without thinking of themselves. They displayed incredible amount of effort, kindness and generosity in bringing us into the world, looking after us, feeding us, taking care of us, tending to our every need, drying our tears, educating us, teaching us language and making us well behaved to be among other people. They have taken care of us so well without expecting anything in return, not even a word of praise. They did their duty to the best of their ability, but many children take their parents for granted. They do not understand the value of their parents and are not grateful to them for the noble service provided.

The Buddha preached that the person who does not acknowledge the blessings of their parents fails and never flourishes. On the other hand a person who shows gratitude to his parents does not fail but definitely flourishes.

The teachings of the Buddha about parents could be found in many of his discourses. He described, what makes the parents the ones called 'first teachers'. That is because they bring us to the world and as the world is being introduced, they teach us how to live in this society with dignity. The Buddha also said 'brahma' is a designation assigned for mother and father. It is said that the brahma is of divine abodes (brahma vihara) such as loving kindness, compassion, empathetic joy (non-jealousy), and equanimity. Parents also have got those four qualities and therefore, they are called   brahma. In the same discourse the Buddha designates parents as 'first deities' and 'gift - worthy'. Why is this? It is because mother and father are very helpful to their children, they take care of them and bring them up and teach them about the world'.

It is not easy to repay parents for their invaluable commitment towards children. The Buddha says that even if a child were to put his or her mother up on one shoulder and father on the other and carry them around for one hundred years while providing them with well-prepared food that they enjoy, bathing and massaging them, allowing them to excrete and urinate right there on the shoulders and giving them huge sums of money, the obligation to parents still could not be fulfilled. Even if you make your parents -universal monarchs-, the rulers of the whole world, it is yet inadequate to show gratitude to parents.

So, children are indebted to their parents for the noble services provided and the Buddha taught how we can repay them. If the parents have little or no faith in the noble Triple Gem (Buddha, Dhamma, Sangha), you establish their confidence in the Triple Gem. If the parents are unvirtuous or do not practise five precepts, you establish them in virtue. If they are stingy, you make them delight in giving. If they have a poor knowledge of Dhamma, you help them to have a good knowledge of Dhamma. If they lack wisdom, you help them to gain wisdom. Therefore, what we need to do in settling what we owe them, is not an ordinary requirement, but a sacred obligation.

The Buddha did not ignore the basic kinds of needs of parents. While helping your parents to gain the above mentioned five wholesome qualities, you should also take care of your parents in the same way they took care of you. There may be a time when they reach old age, fall ill, become bed-ridden and are unable to control their natural body functions. They are obviously helpless at these times, so it is the noble duty of grateful children to attend to their needs. If it is impossible to attend personally, see at least how they can be taken care of. If they suffer from an incurable disease and are dying, console them by preaching Dhamma, remind them about the impermanence of life and establish them in a heavenly world by reminding them of the good deeds done by them. It heals all the pain and bring them peace of mind. It could also be a more effective and powerful medicine.

The Buddha preached that a child should minister to the needs of his parents in five ways.

(i) Having been supported by them I will support them in my turn.

(ii) I will perform their duties for them.

(iii) I will keep up the family tradition.

(iv) I will make myself worthy of my heritage.

(v) I will make offerings, dedicating merits to them after their death.

Sterling qualities of parents are immeasurable and words are insufficient to praise them and their commitment to us. Therefore, let us show our love and gratitude to them and pay our special attention to their spiritual welfare in order for them to get free from this dangerous journey of samsara.

Mother and father are called
'Brahma' 'early teachers'
And 'worthy of gifts'.
Being compassionate towards
Their family of children.

Thus the wise should venerate them,
Pay them due honour
Provide them with food and drink
Give them clothing and a bed
Anoint and bathe them
And also wash their feet.
When he performs such duties
For his mother and father
The wise praise that wise person even here
And thereafter he rejoices in heaven

-*Sabrahmaka Sutta*-

It is a custom of Buddhists to worship parents with the following verses,

Dasa māse urekatvā – Pōsesi uddhi kāranam
Āyu dīgan vassa satam – Mātu pādam namā maham

Mother, I pay my salutation to you for bearing me in your womb for ten months and nurturing me to live hundred years.

Uddhi kāro alingitvā – Chumbitvā piya puttakan
Rāja majjam supatitthan – Pītu pādam namā maham

Father, I pay homage to you for the love showered on me and for the protection and patronage given to stabilise me in the society.

Chapter Twenty

If a person does not find a companion who is better or equal
in qualities, he should resolve to live alone. There is no
fellowship with bad persons.

- *Dhammapada* -

The Noble Friends (Kalyāna Mitta)

Everyone in this world associates with a friend. One may have a wide circle of friends. It is hard to find someone who does not keep company with a friend. Associating a friend is the inherent nature of the human beings and therefore it is seldom that a man is without a friend. Most of the times, a friendship builds up between two when common interests and opinions are found in each other. Success of such association will depend only on the moral quality of these interests and opinions. However, one who follows the teachings of the Supreme Buddha has to be very careful when finding a friend because a friend is a decisive factor in his life.

Being the noblest friend of all the heavenly and human beings, the Supreme Buddha designated a good or true friend as 'Kalyana Mitta', the noble friend. To identify a friend as a noble friend, he should basically have moral conduct. It means a noble friend is one who keeps five precepts, that is; he has refrained from killing living beings, stealing, sexual misconduct, telling lies and taking intoxicating drinks and drugs. While he leads a virtuous life by keeping the five precepts, he establishes his friend as well in those five precepts.

The noble friend admonishes and instructs his friend to get rid of wrong. He protects his friends from misdeeds. The Supreme Buddha said that "if one points out faults and reproves for the best, he is just like one who guides his fellow to a hidden treasure and therefore, one should follow such a wise person. It is always better and never worse to cultivate such an association". Also, the Supreme Buddha in Mitta Sutta pointed out seven factors that a good friend possesses. They are:

1. He gives what is hard to give.
2. He does what is hard to do.
3. He patiently endures what is hard to endure.
4. He reveals his secrets to you.
5. He preserves your secrets.
6. He does not forsake you when you are in trouble.
7. He does not despise when your wealth is running out.

The noble friend shows enormous compassion towards his friends.

If his friends have little or no faith in the noble Triple Gem (Buddha, Dhamma, Sangha), he establishes their confidence in the Triple Gem. If his friends are unvirtuous or do not practise five precepts, he establishes them in virtue. If his friends are stingy, he makes them rejoice in giving. If his friends have a poor knowledge of Dhamma, he helps them to have a good knowledge of Dhamma. If his friends lack wisdom, he helps them to gain wisdom by means of listening to the Dhamma and practising meditation.

It is certainly because of a noble friend that one gets the rare opportunity to listen to the noble teachings (Dhamma) of the Supreme Buddha. As a result, one gets the rare chance to live by the Dhamma and to be free from suffering forever. The association of a noble friend paves the way towards all good, welfare and betterment of a person. When the chief attendant monk, Ānanda commented that a noble friend is the half of the holy life, the Supreme Buddha correcting the comment, stated that a noble friend is the whole of the holy life. This clearly shows the importance of the association of a noble friend for one's life.

It is rarely that one gets the association of noble friends as they are rare in the world. Most of the times, the friends, one gets to associate are not kalyāna mittas but pāpa mittas (evil friends). Just as one's life becomes prosperous and ends up in a happy destination because of a noble friendship, one's life becomes ruined and ends up in a bad destination like hell if he gets into an association of a bad friend. Therefore, the Supreme Buddha most compassionately pointed out who bad friends are in order to get away from them. The Supreme Buddha showed four types of bad friends who can be seen as foes in friendly guise. Their characteristics are as follows.

- The man who is all take.
- The great talker.
- The flatterer.
- The hell-supporter (the man who helps his friend to be born in hell).

The man who is all take is a false friend for four reasons:

- He definitely takes something from his friend.
- He gives very little and wants a lot in return for that.
- He helps his friend only when he is in trouble or fear.
- He associates his friend for his own needs.

The great talker is a false friend for four reasons:

- He talks about favours that could have been done in the past ("If you had told it earlier, I'd have helped you….").
- He talks about favours that will be done in future ("I shall do such and such things for you in the future…").
- He mouths empty words of goodwill.

- When something is needed to be done in the present, he pleads inability owing to some difficulty that he had gone through.

The flatterer is a false friend for four reasons:

- He assents to bad actions.
- He dissents from good actions.
- He praises his friend to his face.
- He speaks ill of his friend behind his back.

The hell-supporter is a false friend for four reasons.
(His companionship leads the other to be born in a bad destination)

- He is friendly when you indulge in intoxicating drinks and drugs.
- He is very friendly when you haunt the streets at unfitting times.
- He is very friendly when you go for music, dancing, dramas and games.
- He is a friend when you indulge in gambling.

(Singalovada Sutta - DN 3)

The Supreme Buddha advised the disciples that "those four friends are really foes, not friends. The wise man recognising this should keep aloof from them as from a fearful path". He reiterated "not to associate with evil companions; not to seek the fellowship of the vile. Associate with good friends; seek the fellowship of noble friends".

(Dhammapada - Pandita Vagga)

Chapter Twenty-One

Give up repenting over the past, give up dreaming of the future, give up being attached to the present. Cross over the existence. Be one who has a mind free from everything. Be one who will not come to the world of birth and decay again and again.

- *Dhammapada* -

Aggañña Sutta

On How the World Began (an extract)

The Supreme Buddha, with His superior knowledge realised how this planet earth comes to an end after a long period of time. Though the physical world is completely destroyed, the beings' 'wandering', the samsaric journey does not come to an end that way. Beings are born in the Ābhassara Brahma world, when the world is destroyed. They are reborn in the human world, when it begins to expand again. The Supreme Buddha, the knower of the world, made a startling disclosure about the expansion of this world after a long period of contraction, the end of the world. Given below is how it happens as is mentioned in Aggañña sutta.

There comes a time, when, sooner or later after a long period, this world contracts. At the time of contraction, beings are mostly born in the Ābhassara Brahma world. And there they dwell, mind-made, feeding on delight, self-luminous, moving through the air, glorious - and they stay like that for a very long time. But sooner or later, after a very long period, this world begins to expand again. At the time of expansion, the beings from the Ābhassara Brahma world, having passed away from there, are mostly reborn in this world. Here they dwell, mind-made, feeding on delight, self-luminous, moving through the air, glorious and they stay like that for a very long time.

At that period, there was just one mass of water, and all was darkness, blinding darkness. Neither moon nor sun appeared, no constellations or stars appeared, night and day were not distinguished, nor months and fortnights, no years or seasons, and no male and female, beings being identified just as beings. And sooner or later, after a very long period of time, savoury earth spread* itself over the waters where those beings were. It looked just like the skin that forms itself over hot milk as it cools. It was endowed with colour, smell and taste. It was the colour of fine ghee or butter, and it was very sweet, like pure wild honey.

Then some being of a greedy nature said: "I say, what can this be?" and tasted the savoury earth on its finger. In so doing, it became taken with the flavour, and craving arose in it. Then other beings, taking their cue from that one, also tasted the stuff with their fingers. They too were taken with the flavour, and craving arose in them. So they began to make balls of the savoury earth with their hands, in order to eat it. And the result of this was that their self-luminance disappeared. And as a result of the disappearance of their self-luminance, the moon and the sun appeared, night and day were distinguished, months and fortnights appeared, and the year and its seasons. To that extent the world re-evolved.

And those beings continued for a very long time feasting on this savoury earth, feeding on it and being nourished by it. And as they did so, their bodies became coarser, and a difference in looks developed among them. Some beings 'became good-looking, others ugly. And the good-looking ones despised the others, saying: "We are better-looking than they are." And because they became arrogant and conceited about their looks, the savoury earth

---

*At that juncture the earth could be eaten as it tasted delicious

disappeared. At this they came together and lamented, crying: "Oh that flavour! Oh that flavour!" And so nowadays when people say: "Oh that flavour!" when they get something nice, they are repeating an ancient saying without realising it.

And then, when the savoury earth had disappeared, a fungus cropped up, in the manner of a mushroom. It was of a good colour, smell, and taste. It was the colour of fine ghee or butter, and it was very sweet, like pure wild honey. And those beings began to eat the fungus. And this lasted for a very long time. And as they continued to feed on the fungus, so their bodies became coarser still, and the difference in their looks increased still more. And the good-looking ones despised the others... And because they became arrogant and conceited about their looks, the sweet fungus disappeared. Next, creepers appeared, shooting up like bamboo..., and they too were very sweet, like pure wild honey.

And those beings began to feed on those creepers. And as they did so, their bodies became even coarser, and the difference in their looks increased still more. And they became still more arrogant, and so the creepers disappeared too. At this they came together and lamented, crying: "Alas, our creeper's gone! What have we lost!" And so now today when people, on being asked why they are upset, say: "Oh, what have we lost!" they are repeating an ancient saying without realising it.

And then, after the creepers had disappeared, rice appeared in open spaces, 'free from powder and from husks, fragrant and clean-grained. 'And what they had taken in the evening for supper had grown again and was ripe in the morning, and what they had taken in the morning for breakfast was ripe again by evening, with no sign of reaping. And these beings began to feed on this rice, and this lasted for a very long time. And as they did so, their bodies became coarser still, and the difference in their looks became even greater. And the females developed female sex-organs, and the males developed male organs. And the women became excessively preoccupied with men, and the men with women. Owing to this excessive obsession with each other, passion was aroused, and their bodies burnt with lust. And later, because of this burning, they indulged in sexual activity.

And those beings who in those days indulged in sex were not allowed into a village or town for one or two months. Accordingly, those who indulged for an excessively long period in such immoral practices began to build themselves dwellings so as to indulge under cover.

Now it occurred to one of those beings who was inclined to laziness: "Well now, why should I be bothered to gather rice in the evening for supper and in the morning for breakfast? Why shouldn't I gather it all at once for both meals?" And he did so. Then another one came to him and said: "Come on, let's go rice-gathering." "No need, my friend, I've gathered enough for both meals." Then the other, following his example, gathered enough rice for two days at a time, saying: "That should be about enough." Then another being came and said to that second one: "Come on, let's go rice-gathering." "No need, my friend, I've gathered enough for two days." (The same for 4, then 8, days). However, when those beings made a store of rice and lived on that, husk-powder and husk began to envelop the grain, and where it was reaped it did not grow again, and the cut place showed, and the rice grew in separate clusters.

And then those beings came together lamenting: "Wicked ways have become widespread among us: at first we were mind-made, feeding on delight... (all events repeated down to the latest development, each fresh change being said to be due to 'wicked and unwholesome ways')... and the rice grows in separate clusters. So now let us divide up the rice into fields with boundaries." So they did so.

Then, one greedy-natured being, while watching over his own plot, took another plot that was not given to him, and enjoyed the fruits of it. So they seized hold of him and said: "You've done a wicked thing, taking another's plot like that! Don't ever do such a thing again!" "I won't", he said, but he did the same thing a second and a third time. Again he was seized and rebuked, and some hit him with their fists, some with stones, and some with sticks. And in this way, taking what was not given, and censuring, and lying, and punishment, took their origin.

Then those beings came together and lamented the arising of these evil things among them: taking what was not given, censuring, lying and punishment. And they thought: "Suppose we were to appoint a certain being who would show anger where anger was due, censure those who deserved it, and banish those who deserved banishment! And in return, we would grant him a share of the rice. "So they went to the one among them who was the most handsomes, the best looking, the most pleasant and capable, and asked him to do this for them in return for a share of the rice, and he agreed.

The Supreme Buddha thus teaches how the title, 'King' was introduced for the first time in the world and further, He explains how the casts system was started in the society. Thus, the world is still undergoing changes until it comes to an end after a long time proving that nothing remains the same and everything is impermanent.

Chapter Twenty-Two

When one looks upon the world as a bubble that is soon broken and as a mirage that soon vanishes, the Mara, the King of Death cannot see.

- Dhammapada -

Appearance of the Seven Suns

The Supreme Buddha who appeared in this world about 2600 years ago understood everything about all the worlds and escaped from all those worlds forever. His knowledge about the worlds is wonderful. Nothing is hidden from His knowledge about the worlds. The true world He saw is not what we call a planet. The true world He saw is spiritual. On one occasion, He named eye, ear, nose, tongue, body and mind as the world because one senses the world as the world with those six sense bases. In reply to a question asked by a god the Supreme Buddha said "The world's end can never be reached by means of travelling. Yet without reaching the world's end, there is no release from suffering. It is in just this fathom-high body endowed with perception and mind that I make known the world, the origin of the world, the cessation of the world and the way leading to the cessation of the world".

What is special about the Buddha's teachings on the world is the fact that everything which belongs to the world is impermanent. Taking up a little lump of cow dung in His hand, He said 'there is not even this much individual thing (in the world) that is permanent, stable, eternal, not subject to change and that will remain the same'.

The Supreme Buddha clearly saw what would happen to the physical world, the Earth because of that impermanence. He said that this great ocean would dry up and the Himalayans, the king of mountains and the great earth would be destroyed completely by fire. How it will happen is mentioned in the Sutta named Sattasuriyodgamana, The Arising of Seven

Suns in Anguttara Nikāya, the Numerical Discourses of the Buddha. The Sutta is as follows.

Seven Suns (Sattha Suriyodgamana Sutta)

On one occasion the Blessed One was dwelling at Vesālī in Ambapālī's Grove. There the Blessed One addressed the bhikkhus: "Bhikkhus!"

"Venerable sir!" those bhikkhus replied. The Blessed One said this:

"Bhikkhus, conditioned phenomena are impermanent; conditioned phenomena are unstable; conditioned phenomena are unreliable. It is enough to become, disenchanted with all conditioned phenomena, enough to become dispassionate towards them, enough to be liberated from them.

"Bhikkhus, Sineru, the king of mountains (the mount range of Himalayans), is 84,000 yojanas in length and 84,000 yojanas in width; it is submerged 84,000 yojanas* in the great ocean and rises up 84,000 yojanas above the great ocean.

"There comes a time, bhikkhus, when rain does not fall for many years, for many hundreds of years, for many thousands of years, for many hundreds of thousands of years. When rain does not fall, seed life and vegetation, medicinal plants, grasses, and giant trees of the forest wither and dry up and no longer exist.

"There comes a time when, after a long time, a second sun appears. With the appearance of the second sun, the small

---

*A yojana is a distance of seven kilometres.

rivers and lakes dry up and evaporate and no longer exist.

"There comes a time when, after a long time, a third sun appears. With the appearance of the third sun, the great rivers— the Ganges, the Yamunā, the Aciravatī, the Sarabhū, and the Mahī dry up and evaporate and no longer exist.

"There comes a time when, after a long time, a fourth sun appears. With the appearance of the fourth sun, the great lakes from which those great rivers originate— Anotatta, Sīhapapāta, Rathakāra, Kaṇṇamuṇda, Kuṇāla, Chaddanta, and Mandākinī[1] dry up and evaporate and no longer exist.

"There comes a time when, after a long time, a fifth sun appears. With the appearance of the fifth sun, the waters in the great ocean sink by a hundred yojanas, two hundred yojanas... three hundred yojanas... seven hundred yojanas. The water left in the great ocean stands at the height of seven palm trees, at the height of six palm trees... five palm trees... four palm trees... three palm trees... two palm trees... a mere palm tree. The water left in the great ocean stands at the height of seven fathoms...[2] six fathoms ... five fathoms... four fathoms... three fathoms... two fathoms... a fathom... half a fathom... up to the waist... up to the knees... up to the ankles. Just as, in the autumn , when thick drops of rain are pouring down, the waters stand in the hoof prints of cattle here and there, so the waters left in the great ocean will stand here and there [in pools] the size of the hoof prints of cattle. With, the

---

[1]These lakes which are situated on the top of the Himalayan mountain range cannot be seen with our naked eyes.

[2]A fathom is a height equal to six feet or 1.8 metres.

appearance of the fifth sun, the water left in the great ocean is not enough even to reach the joints of one's fingers.

"There comes a time when, after a long time, a sixth sun appears. With the appearance of the sixth sun, this great earth and Sineru, the king of mountains, smoke, fume, and smolder. Just as a potter's fire, when kindled, first smokes, fumes, and smolders, so with the appearance of the sixth sun, this great earth and Sineru the king of mountains, smoke, fume, and smolder.

"There comes a time when, after a long time, a seventh sun appears. With the appearance of the seventh sun, this great earth and Sineru, the king of mountains, burst into flames, blaze up brightly, and become one mass of flame. As the great earth and Sineru are blazing and burning, the flame, cast up by the wind, rises even to the brahma world. As Sineru is blazing and burning , as it is undergoing destruction and being overcome by a great mass of heat, mountain peaks of a hundred yojanas disintegrate; mountain peaks of two hundred yojanas... three hundred yojanas... four hundred yojanas... five hundred yojanas disintegrate.

"When this great earth and Sineru, the king of mountains, are blazing and burning, neither ashes nor soot are seen. Just as, when ghee or oil are blazing and burning, neither ashes nor soot are seen, so it is when this great earth and Sineru, the king of mountains, are blazing and burning.

So impermanent are conditioned phenomena, so unstable, so unreliable. It is enough to become disenchanted with all conditioned phenomena, enough to become dispassionate towards them, enough to be liberated from them.

"Bhikkhus, who, except those who have seen the truth, would think or believe is great earth and Sineru, the king of mountains, will burn up, be destroyed, and will no longer exist?"

_____